A Bible Dictionary
for Young Readers

A BIBLE
DICTIONARY
FOR
YOUNG READERS

WILLIAM N. McELRATH

ILLUSTRATED BY DON FIELDS

BROADMAN PRESS
Nashville, Tennessee

ISBN: 0-8054-4404-1
4244-04

Dewey Decimal Number: J220.3
Library of Congress Catalog Card Number 65-15604
Printed in the United States of America

About this book

"I know about Bibles," you may be saying to yourself, "and I know about dictionaries. But what about a *Bible dictionary?* How is it supposed to help me read and study the Bible?"

Maybe a good way to begin answering that question is to turn to your Bible itself. Find the third chapter of the first book in the New Testament.

1. Look over those first few verses of Matthew, chapter 3. You see the names of some persons, don't you? John the Baptist . . . Abraham . . . who were they? This Bible dictionary will tell you.

2. Notice the types or groups of persons mentioned in those verses, too: prophet . . . Pharisees . . . Sadducees. What kind of people were they? Look them up in this book and see.

3. How about places? Can you find three places, all beginning with J, in Matthew 3? Exactly where is Jerusalem? What territory did Judea include? Is "Jordan" the same as that present-day country in the Middle East? No, but the modern nation takes its name from the ancient river. This book not only tells you about places *then;* it tells you about the same places *now*.

4. Persons, places—how about things? There are plenty of things mentioned in the Bible, so there are also many of them listed in this Bible dictionary. In Matthew 3 notice "wilderness," and "locusts," and "vipers," and "chaff." This book will tell you interesting facts about those words.

5. Did you find some unfamiliar or rather old-fashioned words and phrases in Matthew 3? How about "suffer"? What does "at hand" really mean? These and many more are included in this book.

6. How about more familiar words and phrases that have special meanings in the Bible? Can you define "repent"? "kingdom of heaven"? "confessing"?

"sins"? "baptism"? If not, you need this Bible dictionary.

7. Especially tricky are those words that have changed their meanings — since Bible times, or since earlier translations of the Bible were prepared. An example is "leather girdle," in Matthew 3:4. Look up the word "girdle" in this book. Notice also the word "floor" in Matthew 3:12. Not many people of today get the right mental picture of outdoor threshing floors, once so important in preparing grain for use as food. Read the entry for "floor" to get a clearer picture in your mind.

8. Also puzzling are Bible words that have more than one meaning. "Baptize" has two meanings in the same verse: Matthew 3:11. You may find both meanings in this book. (See "baptism.") And for "baptize" and every other word that has more than one meaning, a Bible reference is included in this dictionary with each definition. You may look up the verses and see for yourself the different ways Bible words are used.

9. And then there are words, not in the Bible itself, but important for Bible study. What does it mean to say that Matthew is one of the "Synoptic Gospels"? that Matthew lists Jesus' "Beatitudes"? What does "Trinity" mean — and "ascension" and "Golden Rule"? This book will help you know.

These are just a few of the kinds of help you may find as you use this Bible dictionary. All of them are intended to make the Bible mean more as you read it and study it.

For this Bible dictionary should never be used by itself. Your Bible should always lie open beside it.

Whoever you are, wherever you live, the Bible is the only book that can tell you about God and his people . . . and how you can be one of God's people. The Bible is the only book that is truly inspired by God — and if you're not sure what that means, look up "inspire." (You might look up "inspiration," too.) Then go back and read some more in that inspired Book — not this or any other Bible dictionary, but the Holy Bible itself.

Key to pronunciation

Symbol	Key Words	Symbol	Key Words
a	hat, cat	b	bed, rub
ā	lāte, āble	d	dog, did
ä	fär, cälm	f	fill, off
		g	give, log
e	set, berry	h	hit, hat
ē	sēē, bē	j	joy, edge
		k	kit, make
i	if, sit	l	leaf, all
ī	bīte, fīre	m	my, him
		n	not, son
ō	nō, ōver	p	peg, lap
ô	lông, hôrn	r	rod, fear
		s	see, pass
ōō	tōōl, rūle	t	toy, hat
yoo	mute	v	voice, have
oo	put, book	w	west, always
yoo	u in unite	y	yes, yard
oi	boy, oil	z	zebra, daze
ou	loud, sound	ch	church, bench
		ng	sing, wrong
u	love, up	sh	show, dash
ū	bũrn, tũrn	th	that, path
		zh	s in measure

ə occurs only in unaccented syllables and indicates the sound of
a in atone
e in diver
i in easily
o in collect
u in circus

A heavy accent mark ′ is placed after a syllable that gets a strong accent, as in be-liev-er (bə lēv′ər).
A light accent mark ′ is placed after a syllable that also gets an accent, but of a weaker kind, as in everlasting (ev′ər las′ting).

A

Aaron (er′ ən). Moses' older brother, who was spokesman for the Israelites in the royal court of Egypt (Exodus 4:14). He later became his nation's first high priest, but died before he reached the Promised Land.

abase. To make low or humble (Luke 18:14).

Abba (ab′bə). Aramaic word for a father, often used by children (Mark 14:36; Romans 8:15–16; Galatians 4:6).

Abednego (ə bed′nē gō). One of three young Hebrew captives in Babylon who were thrown into a blazing furnace because they would worship no one but the true God (Daniel 3).

Abel (ā′b'l). Second son of Adam and Eve, who was killed by his jealous brother Cain (Genesis 4).

abhor. To hate or feel disgust for (Romans 12:9).

abide. 1. To stay (Luke 2:8). **2.** To bear, sustain, stand (Malachi 3:2).

Abigail (ab′ə gāl). Wife of Nabal who apologized for her husband's rudeness to David. After Nabal's death, she became David's wife (1 Samuel 25).

Abishai (ə bī′shī). Nephew of David and older brother of Joab; one of David's bravest warriors (2 Samuel 2:18).

abode. Place to stay (John 14:23).

abomination. Something hateful and disgusting.

Abraham (ā′brə ham). Founder of the Hebrew tribe. At first he was called **Abram** (Genesis 11:26). He lived at Ur (now in southern Iraq) about 2000 B.C., but followed God's directions and moved northwestward to Haran, then southwestward to Canaan. God made a covenant with him and promised him a son, though he was already old. Through this promised son, Isaac, he became the forefather of all Jewish people.

Abram (ā′brəm). **Abraham's** name at first (Genesis 17:1–5).

abroad. 1. Outside; out-of-doors (Genesis 15:5). **2.** In public; in many places (Luke 2:17).

Absalom (ab′sa ləm). King David's handsome son who rebelled against his father. During battle his head became caught in an oak tree (2 Samuel 18:9). There he was killed by Joab.

acacia tree and branch

acacia. Tree whose hard, rot-resisting, orange-brown wood was used to make the ark of the covenant and other objects in the tabernacle (Exodus 25–27; 30; 35–38); same as **shittah** and **shittim.**

acceptation. Belief (1 Timothy 1:15; 4:9).

accursed. Under a curse; set aside to be destroyed (Joshua 6:17).

9

Achaia (ə kā′yə). Roman province; now southern Greece (Acts 18:27).

Acts of the Apostles. Usually called simply "Acts," this fifth book of the New Testament tells how Jesus' followers carried out his missionary commands. Dr. Luke wrote this book of History as a sequel to his Gospel. Chapters 1–8 and 10–12 mainly tell about Jesus' eleven surviving apostles and those who worked closely with them. Chapters 9 and 13–28 mainly tell about the apostle Paul and his missionary travels.

Adam (ad′əm). First man; in fact, his very name means "mankind." He and his wife, Eve, disobeyed God and could no longer live the kind of life God had planned for them (Genesis 2–5).

adder. Snake.

adjure. To command.

adoption. Sometimes used in the New Testament to show that God takes Christians into his own family (Romans 8:15–16).

Adria (ā′dri ə). Adriatic Sea (Acts 27:27).

Adullam (ə dul′əm). Cave in the low hills southwest of Bethlehem (now on the Israeli border). Here David and his family and followers hid from jealous King Saul (1 Samuel 22:1–2).

adultery. Act of a married person who is unfaithful to the true husband or wife. The Bible sometimes says that people commit adultery against the true God when they worship other gods (Ezekiel 23:37).

advent. Coming, especially the coming of Christ. His birth is sometimes called the first advent, or coming; his promised return, the second advent, or **second coming** or **appearing.**

adversary. Enemy.

adversity. Trouble.

Aeneas (ə nē′əs). Man at Lydda whom Peter healed of paralysis (Acts 9:32–35).

afflict. To trouble.

affrighted. Afraid.

aforehand. Ahead of time (Mark 14:8).

aforetime. Before (Daniel 6:10); in earlier times (Romans 15:4).

Agabus (ag′ə bəs). New Testament prophet who warned Christians in Antioch about a coming famine (Acts 11:28) and Paul about a coming imprisonment (Acts 21:10–11).

agony. Pain almost too great to bear —of body, of mind, or of both; often especially refers to Jesus' experience in the garden of Gethsemane (Luke 22:44).

Agrippa (ə grip′pə). Herod Agrippa II, a Jewish king under Roman rule. He listened to Paul's legal defense when asked to do so by a Roman governor (Acts 25–26).

Ahab (ā′hab). Brave but wicked king of Israel, the Northern Kingdom. Husband of the still more wicked Queen Jezebel, he was challenged and warned by the prophets Elijah and Micaiah (1 Kings 16–22).

Ahasuerus (ə hazh′oo er′əs). King of Persia who chose Esther as his new queen; believed by some people to be the same king as Xerxes (Esther 1–10).

Aholiab (ə hō′li ab). Same as **Oholiab.**

alabaster. Smooth, cream-colored stone that is often carved into jars (Mark 14:3).

alas (ə las′). Exclamation of sorrow, pity, or fear (Judges 6:22).

Alexandria (al′ig zan′dri ə). Major city of the ancient world, founded in northern Egypt by King Alexander the Great. In New Testament times it was a famous center of learning (Acts 18:24).

alleluia (al'ə lōō'yə). Praise the Lord!

Almighty (ôl mī'ti). Having all might or power; often used as part of a name of God (Revelation 4:8), and sometimes as a separate name: "the Almighty" (Job 11:7).

alms. Offerings, especially for poor people (Acts 3:2–3).

aloes (al'ōz). Oily, fragrant perfume taken from the inner part of a tree.

Alpha and Omega (al'fə and ō mē'gə or ō mā'gə). First and last letters in the Greek alphabet. When used as a name for God, this means "the beginning and the end," or, "everything from *a* to *z*" (Revelation 1:8).

Ammon (am'ən), **Ammonites** (am'ə-nīts). Nation that occupied what is now northern Jordan. Their capital was at the same place as the present capital of Jordan. Usually they were enemies of the Israelites. Babylonia finally destroyed the nation about 580 B.C.

Amorites (am'ə rīts). Tribe that lived at many places in the ancient Middle East. Some of the great kingdoms in the Tigris-Euphrates Valley were founded by Amorites. So were some of the cities conquered by the Israelites in Canaan (Joshua 10:5).

Amos (ā'məs). **1.** Great prophet who

altars for burnt offerings

altar. Place for offering sacrifices—sometimes just a pile of stones (Joshua 8:30–31), sometimes a raised platform (Exodus 27).

Amalek (am'ə lek), **Amalekites** (ə-mal'ə kīts). Tribe of nomads whose forefather was Esau. They roamed what are now northern Saudi Arabia, southern Jordan and Israel, and northeastern Egypt. They tried to block the Israelites' way into the Promised Land, and the two nations were always enemies after that (Exodus 17:8).

amen. Let it be so! This is the truth! (Especially used after prayers.)

amiable. Lovely; lovable (Psalm 84:1).

amiss. Wrong (Luke 23:41); wrongly (James 4:3).

lived about 780–745 B.C. He was a farmer and shepherd at Tekoa (south of Bethlehem), in Judah, the Southern Kingdom. At God's command he prophesied in Israel, the Northern Kingdom. His message was unpopular, but he kept on speaking it. **2.** Third book in the Minor Prophets section of the Old Testament. Amos was the first written of all books of prophecy. Its main theme is the sin of God's people and their need to repent. The book is written partly in prose, partly in colorful poetry.

Amram (am'ram). Father of Moses, Aaron, and Miriam (1 Chronicles 6:3).

Anak (ā'nak), **Anakim** (an'ə kim), **Anakims** (an'ə kimz). Tribe of tall, fierce people who lived in Canaan (Numbers 13:33).

Ananias (an ə nī′əs). **1.** Christian of Jerusalem who was more interested in being praised than in telling the truth (Acts 5). **2.** Christian of Damascus who helped Paul at the time of his conversion (Acts 9). **3.** Cruel high priest who tried Paul (Acts 23).

anathema (ə nath′ə mə). Under a curse; set aside to be destroyed (1 Corinthians 16:22).

Anathoth (an′ə thäth). City of priests, about two miles north of Jerusalem; hometown of the prophet Jeremiah (Jeremiah 1:1). It is now the Jordanian town of 'Anātā.

Andrew (an′drōō). One of Jesus' twelve disciples. He lived at Bethsaida on the Sea of Galilee, and his father's name was Jona or John. First he was a follower of John the Baptist (John 1:40), then of Jesus. He brought to Jesus his brother and partner in the fishing business: Simon Peter.

angel. Heavenly being, especially one sent by God on some special errand—usually to take a message to someone on earth.

an hungered, an hungred. Hungry.

anise (an′is). Plant cultivated for its seeds which were used in seasoning.

Anna (an′ə). Old and widowed prophetess of Jerusalem who recognized the importance of baby Jesus when he was brought to the Temple (Luke 2:36).

Annas (an′əs). Former high priest who was one of the judges at the trial of Jesus (John 18:13).

annunciation. Announcement to Mary that she would become the mother of Jesus (Luke 1:26–38).

anoint. To pour or rub on oil (Psalm 23:5); often part of a ceremony showing that the anointed person is someone special, such as a king (2 Samuel 5:3).

anointed. Person who has been anointed—usually a king or priest (1 Samuel 24:10).

anon. Immediately (Mark 1:30).

antediluvian (an ti di lōō′vi ən). Before the flood described in Genesis 7–8.

antichrist. Great enemy of Christ (1 John 2:18). There are many different ideas as to who or what the antichrist really was, is, or will be.

Antioch in Pisidia (an′ti äk in pi sid′-i ə). City in Galatia (now southwestern Turkey) where Paul preached. He was persecuted there, but started a church (Acts 13–14). This was one of the churches to which he later wrote the letter known as Galatians.

Antioch in Syria (an′ti äk in sir′i ə). Major city of the ancient world, and an early center of Christianity. Now called Antakya, it lies on the Orontes River in south central Turkey. For centuries it was the capital of Syria, known as "Antioch the Beau-

anointing a king

tiful." After the stoning of Stephen, early missionaries took the story of Jesus to Antioch (Acts 11). Jesus' followers were first called Christians there. From there the first foreign missionaries were sent out (Acts 13:1–4).

Antonia (an tō′ni ə). Guard tower (or **castle**) beside the Temple in Jerusalem, where Paul was imprisoned and tried (Acts 21–23).

any wise. Any way (Exodus 22:23).

apocalypse (ə päk′ə lips). Special kind of prophecy, mainly telling about the struggle between God and the powers of evil, in the present and in the future. When "Apocalypse" is capitalized, it usually means the same as **Revelation.**

Apocrypha (ə päk′rə fə). Group of books that used to be included in some Bibles, but now are usually left out. Most Protestants do not believe that they were inspired by God. They contain interesting reading, especially about what happened between the time of the last Old Testament prophet and the time of Christ.

Apollos (ə päl′əs). Christian leader, born in Alexandria, who preached in Ephesus and Corinth (Acts 18: 24).

apostle. Person sent out as a messenger. In the New Testament this usually means either Paul or one of Jesus' twelve closest disciples.

apparel. Clothing.

appearing. In the New Testament, often means the promised return of Christ (Titus 2:13); see **advent.**

apprehend. 1. To capture (Acts 12: 4). **2.** To receive completely, or get in full (Philippians 3:12–13).

approve. To test or prove (2 Timothy 2:15).

Aquila (ak′wə lə). Christian tentmaker who helped Paul at Corinth and Ephesus. He and his wife **Priscilla**

also helped Apollos (Acts 18).

Arabah (ar′ə bə). Great north-south valley that includes the Sea of Galilee, Jordan River, Dead Sea, and canyons running down to the northeastern arm of the Red Sea (Joshua 18:18). Though often called **"plain"** in the Bible (Genesis 13:10–12), it is mostly below sea level.

Arabia (ə rā′bi ə). In the Bible, includes not only what is now Saudi Arabia, but also desert areas to the south and north of it (Galatians 1:17; 4:25).

Aramaic (ar ə mā′ik). Language closely related to Hebrew, the main language of the Old Testament; same as **Syriac.** Ezra 4:8 to 6:18, Ezra 7:12–26, Daniel 2:4*b* to 7:28, and Jeremiah 10:11 are written in Aramaic rather than in Hebrew. Isaiah 36:1–11 tells an interesting story that contrasts the two languages. The few exact, untranslated quotations from Jesus in the New Testament (such as in Mark 5:41; 7:34; 14:36; 15:34) are in Aramaic. It was the usual spoken language for Jesus and his first followers.

Arameans (ar ə mē′ənz). Tribe that lived at many places in the ancient Middle East. Out of them came the Hebrews (see Deuteronomy 26:5), for Abraham was an Aramean. One of the strongest of many Aramean kingdoms was **Syria;** some Bible translations use "Syrians" rather than "Arameans."

Ararat (ar′ə rat). Mountainous area (now in eastern Turkey and southwestern Soviet Union) where Noah's ark landed (Genesis 8:4).

Araunah (ə rô′nə). Jebusite in Jerusalem who sold his outdoor threshing floor to King David as the site for an altar (2 Samuel 24:18–25); same as **Ornan.**

13

archangel (ärk än'jəl). Chief angel (1 Thessalonians 4:16).

Archelaus (är'kə lā'əs). Son of King Herod the Great who succeeded his cruel father as ruler (Matthew 2:22).

Arcturus (ärk toor'əs). Star or constellation, possibly the Big Dipper (Job 9:9; 38:32).

God's invisible presence with his people, and was often called the ark of God, the ark of the Lord, or the ark of the testimony.

Armageddon (är'mə ged'ən). Location of a great battle told about in the book of Revelation (16:16). No one knows exactly where it is.

armor, armour. Covering worn to pro-

Areopagus (Mars' Hill) today.

Paul preaching on Mars' Hill

Areopagus (ar'i äp'ə gəs). Rocky hill in the city of Athens where Paul preached (Acts 17:19); also, a court which met at first on this hill; same as **Mars' Hill.**

Arimathaea, Arimathea (ar'ə mə-thē'ə). Hometown of Joseph, who buried Jesus (Luke 23:51); now in Jordan, northwest of Jerusalem.

ark (ärk). **1.** Huge houseboat which Noah and his sons built at God's command (Genesis 6:14–16). **2.** Tiny basket-boat in which Moses' mother planned to keep her baby safe (Exodus 2:3). **3.** Same as **ark of the covenant** (1 Samuel 7:2).

ark of the covenant. Special sacred chest, built of acacia wood and covered with gold (Exodus 25; 40). Different holy objects were kept in it at different times, especially the stone tablets on which the Ten Commandments were engraved. It was a visible sign of

tect a person against weapons.

armor-bearer, armourbearer. Personal soldier-servant of a general or other important warrior (1 Samuel 16:21).

array (ə rā'). To dress (Luke 23:11).

art. Older form of "are," used with "thou."

Artemis of the Ephesians (är'tə məs əv *thə* i fē'zhenz). Nature goddess worshiped in Ephesus; not the same as the Greek Artemis or the Roman **Diana** (Acts 19:23–41).

artillery. Weapons (1 Samuel 20:40).

Asa (ā'sə). Good and successful king of Judah, the Southern Kingdom (1 Kings 15). He was very sick during the last part of his long reign, and a regent may have had to take his place.

Asaph (ā'saf). Royal musician in King David's time (1 Chronicles 15–16). Several psalms are said to have been written by him. His

14

descendants continued to be musicians in the Temple.

ascend. To go up.

ascension. Rising or moving upward; usually refers to the way Jesus parted from his followers (Luke 24:50–53; Acts 1:6–12).

ascents, song of. Title describing Psalms 120–134. Probably they were so called because religious pilgrims sang them as they ascended to the Temple in Jerusalem. Sometimes the title is translated **song of degrees,** because the pilgrims went up little by little— by **degrees,** therefore.

Asher (ash′ər). A son of Jacob; tribe of Israel occupying territory in Northwestern Canaan.

Asherah (ə shir′ə), **Asherim** (ə-shir′im), **Asheroth** (ə shir′əth). Pagan goddess, and the object used in worshiping her. This object was made of wood, and may have been a pole. Some translations use the word **"grove"** (Judges 6:25–32).

Ashtoreth (ash′tə räth) **Ashtaroth.** Pagan goddess (1 Kings 11:5).

Asia (ā′zhə). In the Bible, nearly always means a Roman province, not a peninsula or a whole continent (Acts 19:10); now western Turkey.

Asia Minor (ā′zhə mī′nər). Peninsula between the Black Sea and Mediterranean Sea; now central and western Turkey.

Asiarch (ā′zhi ärk). Leading citizen of the Roman province of Asia (Acts 19:31).

asp. Poisonous snake, possibly the cobra (Isaiah 11:8).

ass. Donkey (Matthew 21:2–7).

assay. To try (Acts 9:26).

asswage. To go down (Genesis 8:1).

Assyria (ə sir′i ə). One of the great kingdoms of the ancient Middle East; now northern Iraq. From this homeland its kings and soldiers marched out to conquer many other nations, including (in 721 B.C.) Israel, the Northern Kingdom. Assyria had an up-and-down history for centuries. Finally its greatest capital, Nineveh, was conquered by the Medes and Babylonians in 612 B.C., and the proud, cruel nation came to an end.

astonied. Struck dumb with surprise (Daniel 4:19).

astrologer. Person who was thought to predict the future by studying the stars.

asunder. Into separate parts (Mark 10:9).

Athaliah (ath ə li′ə). Wicked queen who seized the throne of Judah, the Southern Kingdom, by killing her own grandsons. She reigned six years, but then was murdered herself (2 Kings 11).

at hand. Close by; soon to come.

Athens (ath′inz). Chief city of Greece, now and in Bible days. Ruins still standing show what a magnificent city it was in New Testament times. Paul preached there, but had less success than at other places (Acts 17:16–34).

athirst. Thirsty (Matthew 25:44).

atonement. 1. Literally, the making of two separate persons "at one,"

or agreed, or friendly. Jesus made atonement so that God and man may be "at one" (Romans 5:11). **2.** Something done to help bring about forgiveness (Exodus 32:30).

atonement, day of. Jewish holy day with special sacrifices and ceremonies (see **scapegoat**) related to God's forgiveness of sin (Leviticus 16). On this one day the high priest entered the most holy place of the tabernacle (and later, of the Temple) to confess the sin of the whole nation and ask forgiveness. Jews still observe this day in early October of each year; they call it Yom Kippur.

attend. To pay attention (Acts 16: 14).

attendance. Attention (1 Timothy 4: 13).

attent. Attentive.

audience. Hearing (Luke 7:1).

Augustus (ə gus'təs). **1.** Roman emperor at the time of Jesus' birth and boyhood (Luke 2:1). **2.** General title for any Roman emperor (Acts 25:25).

author. One who causes or begins (Hebrews 12:2).

avail. To accomplish.

avenge. To do full justice for, whether punishment (2 Kings 9: 7) or reward (Luke 18:7–8); see **vengeance.**

avenger. Relative of a murdered man who felt duty bound to kill the murderer (Joshua 20:3–9); see **vengeance.**

B

Baal (bā'əl *or* bāl), **Baalim** (bā'ə-lim). Nature god or gods, worshiped by the pagan people of Canaan, and sometimes by unfaithful Israelites. The name actually means "Master." and was used at first for more than one god. Later it came to mean the particular god of Canaan who was supposed to bring sun and rain and make the crops grow. "Baalim" is a plural form of "Baal."

Babel (bā'b'l *or* bab'l). Tower which was built in the Tigris-Euphrates valley. Work on it was stopped when God caused the workmen to speak different languages (Genesis 11:1–9). "Babel" itself is the Hebrew word for Babylon (Genesis 10:10). People of Babylon worshiped their god at a tall temple-tower.

Babylon (bab'ə lən). Great capital city of Babylonia. Its ruins lie on both banks of the Euphrates in southern Iraq. Because Babylon was so great and so wicked, its name has sometimes been applied to other great and wicked cities. For instance, in 1 Peter 5:13 and Revelation 17:5, "Babylon" probably means Rome.

Babylonia (bab'əl ō'ni ə). One of the great kingdoms of the ancient Middle East; same as **Shinar;** now southern Iraq. Its history is closely related to that of Assyria. One of Babylonia's most famous kings was Hammurabi, who organized a code of law. The most successful kings, however, came a thousand years later, when Babylonia conquered Assyria (in 612 B.C.), Judah (in 587), and nearly all other countries of the Middle East. But it was not long before Babylonia itself fell (in 539) to the Medes and Persians.

backsliding. Slipping back, especially back to wrong ways of living (Hosea 4:16).

badgers' skins. Leather of some unknown type, used to cover the tabernacle and objects inside it (Numbers 4:5–25). It was not made from the skin of the animal we know as a badger. Some translations say "porpoise skins"; others, "seal skins."

bakemeats. Foods prepared by a baker (Genesis 40:17).

Balaam (bā'ləm). False prophet hired by the king of Moab to pronounce curses against the invading Israelites. Instead, he pronounced blessings (Numbers 22–24).

Balak (bā'lak). King of Moab who tried in vain to get Balaam to pronounce curses against the Israelites who were about to invade his country (Numbers 22:4).

balance for weighing merchandise

balance, balances. Weighing scales.

balm. Gum or resin which could soothe irritation and act as a mild antiseptic. It is not known for sure from what plant it was taken. Often it was associated with Gilead (Jeremiah 8:22), perhaps because it was exported from or through that region.

baptism. 1. Religious act using water as a symbol of being purified and of beginning a new life. Jews baptized Gentiles who wished to become Jews. John the Baptist baptized those who turned away from their sins. (He also baptized Jesus who had not sinned.) Jesus' followers baptized those who became Christians (Romans 6:4) as a symbol of the death, burial, and resurrection of Jesus. **2.** Hard or painful experience; Jesus used baptism as a figure of speech for death (Mark 10:38–39).

baptize. To perform the act of baptism.

Barabbas (bə rab'əs). Robber and murderer whom Governor Pilate set free rather than Jesus.

Barak (bar'ək). One of the Israelite judges. Deborah encouraged him to lead his people to victory against the Canaanites (Judges 4–5).

barbarian. Foreigner (Colossians 3:11).

barbarous. Foreign (Acts 28:2).

bare. Older form of "bore," past tense of "to bear" (1 Peter 2:24).

Barnabas (bär'nə bəs). Early follower of Christ who generously shared the money from the sale of his property on Cyprus (Acts 4:36–37). He and Paul worked together as missionaries in Antioch, Cyprus, and Galatia. Later, Barnabas and Mark did further missionary work in Cyprus.

barrel. Tall clay jar (1 Kings 17:12–16; 18:33).

barren. Not bearing fruit (2 Kings 2:19); childless (Luke 1:7).

Bartholomew (bär thäl'ə myo͞o). One of Jesus' twelve disciples (Luke 6:14). We know almost nothing about him—unless, as many people think, he was the same man as **Nathanael** (John 1:35–51; 21:2).

Bartimaeus (bär tə mē'əs). Blind beggar of Jericho whom Jesus healed (Mark 10:46–52).

Baruch (bar'ək). Jeremiah's faithful secretary. He wrote warnings as the prophet dictated them, and read these aloud in the Temple and in the king's palace (Jeremiah 36).

Barzillai (bär zil'ī). Wealthy old man who gave King David supplies when he was running away from his rebellious son Absalom (2 Samuel 19:32).

Bashan (bā'shən *or* bā'shan). Area east and northeast of the Sea of Galilee (now southwestern Syria). This plateau was famous for oaks (Isaiah 2:13) and cattle (Psalm 22:12; Amos 4:1).

bath. Liquid measure, probably about 5-1/2 gallons (1 Kings 7: 38; Ezekiel 45:10).

Bathsheba (bath shē'bə), **Bathshua** (bath shōō'ə). Beautiful wife of Uriah the Hittite, then of King David. When she caught David's attention, he took her for his own and had Uriah killed. She later became the mother of King Solomon (2 Samuel 11).

Beatitudes (bi at'ə tōōdz *or* bi at'ə-tyōōdz). Statements that a person is blessed, or happy, or fortunate, for a certain reason. The best-known ones are Jesus' Beatitudes, recorded in Matthew 5:3–12.

Beautiful Gate. Magnificent entrance-way into one of the Temple courts, where Peter and John healed a lame beggar (Acts 3:2,10). Probably the gate was 75 feet high, and made of gold, silver, and bronze.

beckon. To make a gesture, especially a downward wave of the hand (Acts 12:17; 21:40).

bed. Sometimes means just a pallet or straw mat (Mark 2:11).

Beelzebub (bē el'zi bub), **Beelzebul** (bē el'zi bul). Used as a name for the devil (Matthew 12:24–27).

Beer-sheba (bir shē'bə). Important city from very early times, located halfway between the southern end of the Dead Sea and the Mediterranean. It was on one of the ancient caravan routes, and was considered the southern limit of Israelite territory: "from Dan to Beer-sheba." Today the Israeli city of Beer Sheva' is an important industrial center.

befall. To happen to, especially in a bad or unfortunate sense (Psalm 91:10).

beget. To become the father of (Matthew 1).

beguile. To deceive, trick, trap (2 Corinthians 11:3).

Behemoth (bi hē'məth). Hippopotamus, or some other large mammal that lives in marshes (Job 40).

behold. 1. To see (Luke 24:39). **2.** Look! (Luke 2:10).

behove. To become necessary for (Luke 24:46).

Belial (bē'li əl). Good-for-nothing, wicked, lawless, untruthful; usually appears in a phrase such as "sons of Belial" (1 Samuel 2:12).

believe. Especially when followed by "in" or "on," often means more than belief that someone really exists, or that someone is really telling the truth. It means trusting one's whole self to Christ or God.

beloved disciple. Usually believed to be the same as **John the Apostle,** but never called by any name in the Bible except **"disciple whom Jesus loved"** (John 13:23; 19:25–27; 20:1–8; 21:7,20–23).

Belshazzar (bel shaz'ər). Son of the last king of Babylonia, who ruled during his father's absence from Babylon (Daniel 5).

benefits. Good gifts (Psalm 103:2).

Benjamin (ben'jə mən). **1.** Youngest of Jacob's twelve sons. His brother Joseph accused him of stealing a silver cup in Egypt, in order to test their older brothers' love and loyalty (Genesis 42–45). **2.** Smallest of the tribes of Israel. Israel's first king came from this little tribe (1 Samuel 9:20–21).

Benjamite (ben'jə mīt). Member of the tribe of Benjamin.

Berea (bi rē'ə). Same as **Beroea.**

Bernice (bər nēs'). Glamorous and immoral sister of King Herod Agrippa II, who sat beside him and listened to Paul's defense (Acts 25–26).

Beroea (bi rē'ə). City of Macedonia (now northern Greece) where Paul preached; same as **Berea.** Many Jews there studied the Old Testament for themselves, to see whether Paul was telling the truth about prophecies of the Christ (Acts 17:10–14).

beseech. To beg (Romans 12:1).

beset. To attack from all sides (Hebrews 12:1).

besiege. To encircle a city in battle and try to starve it out (Deuteronomy 28:52).

bestow. 1. To put or place (Luke 12:17). **2.** To give (1 John 3:1).

Bethabara (beth ab'ə rə). Place where John the Baptist baptized (John 1:28); thought by many people to be the same as **Bethany,** definition **2.**

Bethany (beth'ə ni). **1.** Small village about 1-5/8 miles east of Jerusalem, on the eastern slope of the Mount of Olives. Jesus visited it many times, often traveling from there to Jerusalem. His special friends lived there— Mary, Martha, and Lazarus. Modern Jordanian inhabitants of the town have renamed it after Lazarus—Al Ayzarīyah. **2.** Place east of the Jordan and a few miles north of the Dead Sea, where John the Baptist baptized. Many of the oldest copies of the New Testament have "Bethany" rather than **"Bethabara"** in John 1:28. The

spot is now in Jordan.

Bethel (beth'el). Famous Israelite city and center of worship; its very name means "house of God." It is mentioned more often in the Old Testament than any other place except Jerusalem. The city lay about 11 miles north of Jerusalem (now in Jordan). Abraham and Jacob worshiped there (Genesis 12:8; 28:11–22). The ark of the covenant was kept there for a time (Judges 20:27). When the Northern Kingdom split off, Bethel marked its southern boundary. King Jeroboam again made it a center of worship, and it was still that in the time of Amos.

Bethesda (be thez'də). Same as **Beth-zatha.**

Bethlehem (beth'li əm *or* beth'li-hem'). Town about 6 miles south of Jerusalem; birthplace of David and of Jesus. Much of the story of Ruth took place there. There David kept his sheep and was anointed king by Samuel. The prophet Micah predicted that the Christ would be born there (Micah 5:2), and he was (Luke 2:1–7). It is now the Jordanian town of Bayt Laḥm.

Bethphage (beth'fə ji). Village east of Jerusalem where Jesus sent two disciples to bring the donkey on which he rode into the city.

Beth-saida (beth sā'ə də). City near the Jordan River where it flows into the northern end of the Sea of Galilee. One fourth of Jesus' disciples came from there (John 1:44; 12:21); yet, few others there seem to have listened to his teaching (Matthew 11:21; Luke 10:13). Some people think there was another Beth-saida on the northwestern shore of the Sea of Galilee, but this seems unlikely. Beth-saida was sometimes called

Julias in honor of the daughter of Emperor Augustus Caesar. Its location is now on the Israeli-Syrian border.

Beth-shan (beth'shan *or* beth shan'), **Beth-shean** (beth shē'an). One of the more important Old Testament cities in the Jordan valley, although mentioned very few times in the Bible (1 Samuel 31:10–12). It is now the Israeli village of Beit Shean.

Bethuel (Be thu'el). Father of **Rebekah** (Genesis 24:24).

Beth-zatha (beth zā'thə). Pool in Jerusalem where Jesus healed a sick man. Many of the oldest copies of the New Testament have "Beth-zatha" instead of **"Bethesda"** in John 5:2.

betimes. Early.

betray. To trick; to turn over to an enemy; to give away a secret.

betroth. To engage to be married.

bettered. Improved.

betwixt. Between.

bewray. To betray.

beyond Jordan. This and similar expressions always mean "on the eastern side of the Jordan," except in Genesis 50:10–11; Deuteronomy 3:20,25; 11:30. In those verses, "on the western side of the Jordan" is meant.

beyond the river. This and similar expressions always mean "on the eastern side of the Euphrates," except in some translations of Ezra and Nehemiah, where "on the western side of the Euphrates" is meant.

Bezaleel (bi zal'i əl), **Bezalel** (bez'ə-lel). Chief craftsman who worked on the tabernacle and its equipment, including the ark of the covenant (Exodus 35–38).

Bible (bī'b'l). Collection of books that make up the inspired Word of God. The word itself means "little

books"—therefore, many books in one. All Jews and Christians call 39 Old Testament books "the Bible." All Christians also call 27 New Testament books "the Bible."

bid. 1. To tell (Joshua 6:10). **2.** To invite (Matthew 22:3).

bier. Stretcher on which bodies were carried to be buried.

birthright. Special rights (such as inheriting a larger share of the father's property and sitting in the most important place at the table) which usually belonged to the first-born son. See Genesis 25:24–34; 43:33.

bishop. Pastor or leader of a church (Titus 1:7).

bishopric. Place of trust or responsibility (Acts 1:20).

bitter herbs. Bitter-tasting green salad eaten at the Passover to remind the Hebrews of their bitter hardships as slaves in Egypt (Exodus 12:8).

bitumen. Asphalt (Exodus 2:3).

blaspheme. To curse or speak bad things about someone, especially about God (Romans 2:24).

blast. To blight or mildew crops (Genesis 41:6).

blemish. Flaw; defect.

bless. Verb that has at least three similar but different meanings in the Bible. Genesis 14:19–20 gives good examples of these three meanings, in the order listed here: **1.** To wish good things for a fellow human being, especially good things from God. **2.** To give good things or show kindness (used only when God so acts toward man). **3.** To praise or worship God.

blessed. 1. Past tense of the verb, "to bless" (Genesis 1:28). **2.** Happy or fortunate (Matthew 5:3–12).

blessing. 1. Good gifts from God

(Deuteronomy 16:17). **2.** Request for God to bless someone, believed to have special power in influencing God (Numbers 6:22–26). **3.** Announcement that God has blessed and will bless someone; also believed to have special power, and to be unchangeable when once spoken (Genesis 27:33–38). Fathers often pronounced blessings on their sons (Genesis 49:1–2,28), especially their eldest sons (Genesis 27:1–4).

blood. Thought by the Hebrews to be, in some special sense, that which gave life to any living thing (Leviticus 17:11). When New Testament writers spoke of Christ's blood, they were often thinking of the sacrifice of his life (Romans 5:9–10).

bloody flux. Dysentery; severe diarrhea (Acts 28:8).

Boanerges (bō'ə nŭr'jēz). Name given by Jesus to James and John, two of his disciples (Mark 3:17). It means "sons of thunder."

Boaz (bō'az). Kind and wealthy landowner in Bethlehem, who let Ruth glean in his fields, and later married her. He was an ancestor of David (Ruth 2).

body. In the New Testament, often means the church, or all Christians everywhere (Romans 12:5). Paul speaks of Christ as the head of this body (Colossians 1:18).

bond. **1.** Imprisoned or enslaved (Galatians 3:28). **2.** Chain or rope (Acts 25:14).

bondage. Imprisonment or slavery (Exodus 1:14).

book. Scroll—the only type of book known in Bible times.

booth. Temporary shelter of poles and branches.

Booths, Feast of (fēst' əv bōo*thz'* or bōoths'). One of the three great annual festivals of the Hebrews; also known as **Tabernacles** and **Ingathering.** It came in October, as a time of thanking God for the harvest, and of praising him for bringing the Israelites through their forty years in the desert. People made and lived in booths to remind themselves of how their nomad ancestors had lived. Other features of the nine-day festival included torchlight ceremonies,

family observing Feast of Booths

21

sunrise services, processions to bring water and pour it out on an altar, waving of branches, and shouts of "Hosanna!" (See Leviticus 23:33–44; Deuteronomy 16: 13–17; Nehemiah 8:13–18; John 7:2,14,37–39.

born again. Born spiritually; a phrase (similar to **new birth** and **regeneration**) describing someone who has been converted or become a Christian (John 3:3–8).

borne. Past participle of "to bear" (Matthew 23:4).

bosom. 1. Breast (Ruth 4:16). **2.** Person's inner feelings; his mind and heart (Ecclesiastes 7:9).

bottle. Animal skin used to hold liquids (Mark 2:22).

bound. 1. Tied or chained (Genesis 42:19). **2.** Boundary (Exodus 23: 31).

bountifully. Generously (2 Corinthians 9:6).

bowels. 1. Any inner part of someone or something (Psalm 71:6). **2.** Person's feelings or attitudes; his mind and heart (1 John 3:17).

box. Stone or clay jar (Mark 14:3).

Branch. Sometimes used as a description of the Saviour whom God promised to send. David's kingdom had been cut off, but a new Branch would grow out and become an everlasting kingdom (Isaiah 11:1; Jeremiah 23:5).

brasen. Bronze.

brass. Bronze.

breach. Broken place, as in a city wall (Amos 9:11).

bread of the Presence. Twelve loaves of fine wheat bread, always kept on a golden table in the tabernacle or Temple. Therefore, it was always in the "Presence" of God in a special way (1 Samuel 21:6; Matthew 12:3–4). It was also called **shewbread** or **showbread,** and was used as one way of showing thanks to God. When new bread was placed on the table each sabbath day, priests ate the old.

breastpiece. Pocket worn on the chest. The high priest had a special breastpiece decorated with twelve jewels set in gold, each bearing the name of one tribe of Israel. Inside the pocket he carried the sacred objects used in finding God's will (Exodus 28); see **lots** and **Thummim.**

breastplate

breastplate. 1. Same as **breastpiece** (Exodus 28). **2.** Piece of metal in a soldier's armor that protected his chest and throat; sometimes called "heart-protector" (Ephesians 6:14).

brethren. Brothers.

bride. Sometimes means the church (all Christians), with Christ being the bridegroom (2 Corinthians 11:2; Revelation 21:9–27).

brimstone. Sulphur.

buckler. Small, round shield, carried in the hand or on the arm (1 Chronicles 5:18).

buffet. To hit, slap, or shove (Matthew 26:67).

builded. Older form of "built" (Proverbs 24:3).

bullock. Young bull.

bulrushes

bulrush. Tall reed that grows in marshes; in Exodus 2:3, the papyrus plant is meant.

burden. Unfavorable or warning prophecy; see Nahum 1:1; Habakkuk 1:1; Malachi 1:1.

burning bush. Object God used in speaking to Moses (Exodus 3:1–6); may have been a thorn bush.

burnt offering, burnt sacrifice. One of the important religious ceremonies of the Hebrews. A worshiper brought some living creature—bull, sheep, goat, dove, or pigeon, according to his wealth. He laid his hands on it as a way of saying, "This creature is taking my place. I am giving all of it on God's altar, as a sign that all of me belongs to God." The creature was then killed and entirely burned. (See Leviticus 1; Romans 12:1; also, **sacrifice.**)

bushel. Measuring vessel that actually held only about 1/4 of an American bushel (Matthew 5:15).

butler. High royal official who took special charge of what the king drank; similar to **cupbearer** (Genesis 40).

butter. Usually means curdled milk —more like cottage cheese than like butter as known today (Genesis 18:8). Curds was considered a tasty dish.

byword. Person or thing thought of as typical of something bad (1 Kings 9:7).

Caesar (sē′zər). Family name taken as a title by all Roman emperors.

Caesarea (ses′ə rē′ə). Great seaport city of Roman times, about 23 miles south of Mount Carmel. It, rather than Jerusalem, was the Roman capital for that area. Peter witnessed to Cornelius there, and there Paul was tried and imprisoned for two years. Only ruins remain now—some on the northwestern coast of Israel, some under the Mediterranean Sea.

Caesarea Philippi (ses′ə rē′ə fil′ə pī). City on a lovely plateau overlooking the northern end of the Jordan River Valley (now on the Israeli border). Near there Peter identified Jesus as "the Christ, the Son of the living God" (Matthew 16:13–17).

buckler

Caiaphas (kā'ə fəs). High priest at the trial of Jesus (Matthew 26:3).

Cain (kān). Oldest son of Adam and Eve, who became jealous of his own brother Abel and killed him (Genesis 4).

Caleb (kā'ləb). One of the twelve spies sent to scout the land of Canaan. Only he and Joshua believed that the Israelites could conquer the land. They were rewarded for their faith by becoming the only grown-ups of their generation who entered the Promised Land (Numbers 13–14.)

calling. 1. Occupation (1 Corinthians 7:20). **2.** Summons or command from God (Philippians 3:14).

call upon. To pray to and believe in (Romans 10:12–13).

Calvary (kal'və ri). Same as **Golgotha.**

Cana (kā'nə). Village in Galilee, about 9 miles north of Nazareth. Here Jesus attended a wedding feast. Present-day ruins (in Israel) are called Khirbet Qānā.

Canaan (kā'nən). Mainly the area between the Jordan River and the Mediterranean Sea, especially before it was conquered by the Israelites; same as the **Promised Land.** This region is now divided among Lebanon, Jordan, and Israel.

Canaanites kā'nə nīts). Tribe that lived in the land of Canaan until they were conquered by the Israelites. They were close kin to the Amorites and the Phoenicians. They worshiped gods such as Baal in wild and wicked ways. The Israelites were supposed to have nothing to do with such religions, but some were influenced by the few Canaanites who stayed in the area.

Cananaean (kā'nə nē'ən). **"Zealot"** —the name of a political and religious party to which Simon (not Peter), one of Jesus' twelve dis-ciples, belonged. Sometimes he is called "Simon the Canaanite," but probably Cananaean is the correct word.

candle. Same as **lamp;** there were no candles in Bible times.

candlestick. Same as **lampstand** (Exodus 25:31–35).

canon. Official list of books of the Bible. The word itself means rule or standard. Believers in God (both Jews and Christians) tried to decide, with God's help, which books truly met God's standards, and so could be called the written Word of God. The five books of Law were the first to be canonized, or recognized as Scripture. The other Old Testament books were canonized later. Jesus and his disciples had only the Old Testament, but books written by such Christians as Paul quickly came to be recognized as Scripture. Except for deciding whether to leave the Apocrypha in or out, the canon of the entire Bible was agreed upon by about 400 years after Christ.

Canticles. Same as **Song of Solomon.**

Capernaum (kə pūr'ni əm). City on the northwestern shore of the Sea of Galilee. Jesus moved there at the beginning of his ministry, and it was his headquarters for the rest of his earthly life. Many stories told in the Gospels took place there; yet, few of its people followed Jesus (Luke 10:15). The site, now in Israel, is called Tell Hum.

captain of the Temple. Priest in the Temple at Jerusalem, second in command to the high priest. One of his duties was to lead the squads of Levites who acted as Temple police (Acts 4:1).

captivity. Condition of being held as a prisoner or an exile; usually refers to the period when people of

Israel, the Northern Kingdom, were exiled in Assyria (beginning between 740 and 721 B.C.), and people of Judah, the Southern Kingdom, were exiled in Babylonia (beginning between 605 and 587 B.C.).

careful. **1.** Anxious; full of care (Philippians 4:6). **2.** Cautious; taking care (Titus 3:8).

Carites (kar'īts). Same as **Cherethites and Pelethites.**

Carmel (kär'məl). **1.** Village in Judah (now in Jordan), south of Bethlehem and west of the Dead Sea, where Nabal held a sheep-shearing festival (1 Samuel 25). **2.** Long mountain that juts northwestward from Galilee to the Mediterranean Sea. Its greatest height is 1,742 feet. There Elijah had his contest with the prophets of Baal. Mount Carmel is famous for the rich, beautiful growth of plants that covers it, even when other nearby areas have dried up. Haifa, modern Israel's chief port, is at the foot of Mount Carmel.

carnal. **1.** Material or earthly, as opposed to spiritual or heavenly (2 Corinthians 10:4). **2.** Relating to human nature when it is under the command of lower impulses or drives, rather than under the command of Christ (1 Corinthians 3:3).

carnally. **1.** In the Old Testament, always means sexually. **2.** In the New Testament, always means worldly, unspiritually, thinking only of matters relating to one's body (Romans 8:6).

carriage. Baggage (1 Samuel 17:22).

cast (kast). **1.** To throw or drop (Acts 27:19). **2.** To mold or shape (Exodus 37:13). **3.** To lose a baby at birth or fruit at harvest time (Genesis 31:38; Malachi 3:11). **4.** To consider (Luke 1:29).

castle. In the book of Acts, same as **Antonia.**

cedar of Lebanon

cedar. Huge, many-trunked cedar trees on the mountains of Lebanon were the main sources of cedar wood in Bible times. This sweet-smelling, sturdy wood was much used in building ships and houses. The cedar came to be a symbol for strength, glory, and beauty. A few of these great trees still grow in northern Lebanon.

Cedron (ked'rən). Same as **Kidron.**

celestial. Heavenly.

censer. Ladle or shovel for carrying live coals from an altar, and for burning incense.

censer

25

centurion

centurion. Roman officer, commander of one hundred men. This was the highest rank an ordinary soldier could reach. It was of great importance in the organized fighting strength of the Roman army. Centurions often had high intelligence and wide experience. They are mentioned more often in the New Testament than are officers of any other rank.

Cephas (sē'fəs). Name meaning "stone," given by Jesus to Simon Peter (John 1:42). The Aramaic name Cephas is the same as the Greek name **Peter.**

chaff. Coarse, inedible husks of wheat, blown away by the wind when the grain is **winnowed.** In the Bible, chaff is always used as a figure of speech for something bad or worthless.

Chaldea (kal dē'ə). Area in the extreme southern tip of the Tigris-Euphrates Valley (now Kuwait and southeastern Iraq).

Chaldeans (kal dē'ənz), **Chaldees** (kal dēz'). **1.** Tribe that lived in Chaldea. They fought against the Babylonians, their neighbors to the north. Finally a Chaldean family gained the throne of Babylonia, and the two countries became one until the fall of Babylonia in 539 B.C. **2.** Members of the Chaldean tribe who, after the fall of their kingdom, became famous as magicians in many parts of the world (Daniel 2:2).

chamberlain. Important officer in a royal court or royal city.

chancellor. Important officer in the royal court of Persia.

change of raiment. Man's robe for special occasions.

changer. Same as **money changer** (John 2:15).

charger (char'jer). A large platter or dish.

chariot. Light, open, two-wheeled cart, usually pulled by two horses. It was used as a status symbol (Genesis 41:43) and as a means of ordinary transportation (Acts 8:28–29,38), but above all, as a battle wagon. One reason David and Solomon won so many victories was that they were the first Hebrew leaders to make much use of war chariots.

charity. Unselfish love (1 Corinthians 13).

chasten. To punish in order to make better.

chastise. To punish, especially by beating.

Cherethites and Pelethites (ker'ə thīts ənd pel'ə thīts). Special foreign bodyguard or personal army hired by David and the kings who succeeded him; same as **Carites.**

Cherith (ker'əth). Brook east of the Jordan River, where Elijah was told to hide (1 Kings 17:3); no one knows which of many streams in Jordan or Syria it is.

cherub, cherubim, cherubims. Type of angel, probably thought of as having a human face, two or four wings, and an animal's body.

chide. To argue or disagree.

chief captain. In the book of Acts, same as **tribune.**

chief priest. Usually means the same as **high priest.**

children. Often means descendants or people (Exodus 1:7).

Chimham (kim′ham). Son of Barzillai, who went in his father's place to live at King David's court (2 Samuel 19:31–40).

Chinnereth (kin′ə reth), **Chinneroth** (kin′ə räth). Same as **Galilee, Sea of** (Joshua 12:3; 13:27).

chode. Old form of "chided," past tense of "to chide."

chosen people. Israelites, Hebrews, or Jews, whom God chose for a spe-

Christ (krīst). Title (not really a name in the usual sense) of Jesus. It means the Anointed One—that is, the one whom God has chosen for a special purpose and honored as in the anointing ceremony for a king or priest. Christ, a Greek word, is the same as **Messiah** (or **Messias**), a Hebrew word (John 1:41). (See **Jesus.**)

Christian (kris′chən). Believer in and follower of Christ. The name appears only three times in the Bible: Acts 11:26; 26:28; 1 Peter 4:16. Jesus' followers "were called Christians first in Antioch" (in Syria). Some people think the name was at

war chariot

cial purpose; sometimes called **people of God** or **people of the Lord.** God first chose Abraham (Genesis 12), then enlarged his choice to all of Abraham's descendants (Exodus 19). He intended that his chosen people should share their knowledge of him with the whole world. Jesus, the Saviour of the world, was born on earth as one of the chosen people. He then began a new chosen people, including anyone—Jew or Gentile—who would follow him (1 Peter 2:9–10).

first used in fun by non-Christians, and only later taken up by Christians. It actually means Christ's man, or member of Christ's party.

Chronicles, 1 and 2 (fŭrst′ ənd sek′-ənd krän′i k'lz). Two books of the Old Testament, usually considered as books of History. The Hebrews placed them in the section called Writings. Chronicles gives a brief history from the beginning of mankind to the time of King David, then a detailed history of Judah, the Southern Kingdom. It includes many stories not found in the books of Samuel and Kings, also some details not found in stories recorded in both places. These details show the purpose of the man or men who were inspired to write Chronicles: to point out the greatness of God, and the way he controls the events of history to work out his purpose.

church. 1. Group of baptized believers in Christ, gathered together at a particular place (Romans 16:1–5). **2.** All Christians of all times and places (Ephesians 5:23–27).

cieled (sēld). Paneled (Haggai 1:4).

Cilicia (si lish′ə). Mountainous and coastal area, divided between two Roman provinces, in what is now south central Turkey. Paul was a native of Cilicia (Acts 22:3), and later a missionary there (Acts 15:40–41).

circumcise. To cut off the foreskin of; done to all Hebrew boy babies at the age of eight days (Genesis 21:4) as a sign of the covenant between God and his people. Jesus was circumcised (Luke 2:21), but his followers realized that this act was no longer a religious necessity (1 Corinthians 7:19).

circumcision. 1. Act of being circumcised (John 7:22–23). **2.** Belief that a person should be circumcised in order to become a Christian (Galatians 2:12).

circumspectly. Carefully (Ephesians 5:15).

city of David. 1. In the Old Testament, Jerusalem—especially the part of it David built on Mount Zion (2 Samuel 5:7). **2.** In the New Testament, Bethlehem—so called because it was David's hometown (Luke 2:4,11).

city of refuge. City where a person who had accidentally killed someone could be safe from the ven-

geance of the dead man's relatives. There were six cities of refuge, three on each side of the Jordan River.

clave (klāv). Old past tense of "to **cleave.**"

clean. Often means, not the opposite of dirty, but the opposite of tabooed (1 Samuel 20:25–26). A person might become **unclean,** or **defiled,** or **polluted,** or tabooed, by releasing (on purpose or accidentally) one of the fluids in his body, by eating certain foods that were taboo, by taking the disease of leprosy, or by touching a corpse. He could become clean again **(purified)** by going through certain ceremonies.

cleave 1. To cut or tear apart (Psalm 141:7). **2.** To stick or become fastened (Deuteronomy 11:22).

Cleopas, Cleophas (klē′ə pəs). One of two men who walked with Jesus to Emmaus on the day Jesus arose from death (Luke 24:18).

close (klōs). Besides the usual definitions, sometimes means quiet (Luke 9:36).

closet. Private room (Matthew 6:6).

clouted. Wrapped with rags (Joshua 9:5).

cloven. Split; divided.

coast. Any area, especially any near a boundary line (Acts 26:20).

cockatrice. Poisonous snake (Isaiah 11:8).

codex. Book written on sheets attached together at one side; not a book written on a scroll. The oldest codex Bibles were written by hand about A.D. 325.

cohort. One tenth of a legion in the Roman army—usually about 600 soldiers; sometimes called band.

college. Newer part of Jerusalem in Old Testament times (2 Kings 22:14).

Colossae, Colosse (kə läs′ə). City of

Asia (in what is now southwestern Turkey) where a Christian church was founded in early times. It was an important river port and textile manufacturing city. Only ruins remain today.

Colossians (kə läsh'ənz). Letter written by Paul to the church at Colossae. He warned his Colossian friends against certain false teachings, told them more about the Christian way of life, encouraged them to live and work together in love, and sent them news of Christians in Rome and greetings to Christians in Colossae. Paul probably wrote the letter while he was under house arrest in Rome (Acts 28:16).

comeliness. Attractive appearance (Isaiah 53:2).

comely. Pleasant.

come to pass. To happen.

comfortably. With words of comfort or encouragement (Isaiah 40:2).

Comforter. Name for the **Holy Spirit** (John 14:26), meaning that he gives Christians comfort, strength, and advice.

commend. To show or prove (Romans 5:8).

commune. To discuss or think about (Luke 6:11).

communicate. To share by giving offerings (Hebrews 13:16).

codex

communion. Sharing; often used to mean the Lord's Supper, in which Christians share with Christ and with one another (1 Corinthians 10:16).

company. Group.

compass. To encircle (Hebrews 12:1).

compassion. Pity, love, mercy.

conceit. Idle thought (Romans 12:16).

concord. Harmony; friendship.

concourse. Assembly (Acts 19:40).

concubine. Slave woman who became a sort of lowly ranked wife in a harem.

condemn. To find to be wrong or guilty.

coney. Probably the rock badger (Proverbs 30:26).

confess. Often means, not just to admit something, but to announce publicly one's intention to follow Christ (Matthew 10:32).

confound. To confuse or cause to be ashamed.

congregation. Assembly of people, especially for religious purposes; the people of Israel.

conquest. Act of conquering; often refers especially to the Israelites' conquest of Canaan, led by Joshua.

consecrate. To separate or set aside someone or something for the service or worship of God (2 Chronicles 29:31, 33).

consolation. 1. Comfort (2 Corinthians 1:5). 2. Salvation (Luke 2:25).

constrain. To persuade (Acts 16:15).

contemn. To despise.

contrite. Humble and sorry for sin.

convenient. 1. Timely (Mark 6:21). 2. Suitable (Ephesians 5:4).

conversation. Behavior (Philippians 1:27).

conversion. Turning or returning; especially, turning toward Jesus and his way of life (Acts 15:3). (See **convert.**)

convert. To turn someone toward God and the right way of life

(James 5:20); to be converted means to repent and trust Jesus as Lord and Saviour (Acts 3:19).

convince. 1. To make someone feel sure (Acts 18:28). 2. To convict or prove guilty (John 8:46).

convocation. Assembly, especially a religious one.

corban (kôr′ban). Set aside as a gift to God (Mark 7:11).

coriander (ko ri an′dər). A herb used to season food.

Corinth (kôr′ənth or kär′ənth). Great Greek city and capital of the Roman province of Achaia. Corinth lay on a narrow neck of land, with the sea on each side. Corinth was a center of wickedness and false worship—so much so that "to corinthianize" meant to make something bad or dirty. Yet, Paul and other missionaries were able to win many Corinthians to Christ.

Corinthians, 1 and 2 (fŭrst′ ənd sek′ənd kə rin′thi ənz). Letters written by Paul to the Christians of Corinth. As one might expect, a church in such a wicked city had many problems. Paul's letters were intended to help with some of these matters and to give good advice on what to believe and how to live. Great passages—about Christian love (1 Corinthians 13), resurrection (1 Corinthians 15), and giving (2 Corinthians 8–9)—help to make these among the most important of New Testament books.

corn. Any kind of grain, such as wheat or barley (John 12:24); American corn was unknown in Bible times.

Cornelius (kôr nēl′yəs). Roman centurion in Caesarea who worshiped the true God. Directed by a vision, he sent for Peter, who led him to become a Christian. He was the first (or first well-known) non-Jew to follow Christ (Acts 10).

cornet. In some translations means ram's horn or shophar.

corruptible. That which will sooner or later rot or waste away.

council. In the New Testament, usually means the same as Sanhedrin (Matthew 26:59).

Counsellor, counselor (koun′s'l ər). Someone who gives advice or counsel; sometimes used as a name for God's promised Messiah (Isaiah 9:6) and for the Holy Spirit (John 14:26 in some translations).

countenance. Face.

court. Walled but unroofed area around or in front of a building. The Temple had several courts, often mentioned in the Psalms.

cousin. Sometimes means any relative (Luke 1:36,58).

covenant. Agreement between two persons or groups. In the Bible, the word usually refers to the agreement between God and his special chosen people—Abraham and his descendants. God agreed to take care of the Israelites as long as they kept their part of the agreement: to serve and worship God alone. Jesus introduced a new covenant, based on faith, and intended for all people (Hebrews 8:6).

covet. To want more than one has—especially, to want greedily what belongs to someone else.

crawling things. Same as creeping things.

creation. Act of making or bringing into being; especially, God's making of everything that exists.

creature. Any living being made by God (2 Corinthians 5:17); all living beings (Romans 8:19–21).

creeping things. Reptiles, insects, or other living beings; same as crawling things.

Crete (krēt). Large Greek island in the eastern Mediterranean Sea.

Crispus (kris'pəs). **Ruler of the synagogue** among the Jews of Corinth, who became a Christian and was baptized by Paul (Acts 18:8; 1 Corinthians 1:14).

cross. 1. Upright stake, usually with a crosspiece, on which Romans nailed or tied criminals and left them to die (John 19:17). **2.** Symbol of giving one's self completely to Christ—being willing even to die for him (Luke 9:23).

crucifixion. Act of putting someone to death by nailing or tying him to a cross; refers especially to the execution of Jesus in this way. Roman crucifixion was the most shameful, painful, and lingering way to die. Only slaves and foreigners—not Roman citizens, no matter what their crime—were killed in this way.

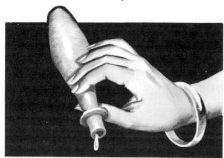

cruse

cruse. Small clay jug, 4 to 6 inches tall, used to hold olive oil.

cubit. Unit of measurement—from one's elbow to the tip of his middle finger, or about 18 to 21 inches.

cumber. 1. To take up space uselessly (Luke 13:7). **2.** To burden down with work (Luke 10:40).

cummin (kum'min). A plant whose seeds were used for seasoning foods.

cunning. 1. Skilful (Exodus 35:35). **2.** Skill (Psalm 137:5).

cup. Sometimes used as a figure of speech for something hard or painful to do (Matthew 26:39).

cupbearer. Court official who serves the king wine and may discuss important matters with him (Nehemiah 1:11); similar to **butler.**

curious. 1. Intricate; done in a skilful, detailed way (Exodus 35:32). **2.** Magic (Acts 19:19).

curse. Announced hope that bad may come to someone or something, or a call upon God to bring bad. A curse was a serious matter to people of Old Testament times; like its opposite, a blessing, it was believed to be almost unchangeable after once spoken.

custom. 1. Usual thing to do (Luke 4:16). **2.** Type of tax (Matthew 9:9).

Cyprus (sī'prəs). Large island in the eastern Mediterranean Sea. As a source of copper, Cyprus (called Chittim or Kittim) was important even in early Old Testament times. It was also important as an early center of Christianity. Barnabas came from there, and returned there as a missionary. Paul, Mark, and others also preached on Cyprus.

Cyrus (sī'rəs). Great Persian king and founder of the Persian empire. He conquered Babylonia in 539 B.C. and allowed some of the exiled Jews to go back home to Jerusalem.

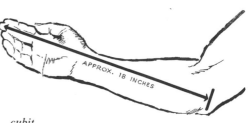

cubit

D

Dagon (dā′gən). God worshiped by the Philistines.

Damascus (də mas′kəs). Capital of Syria and one of the oldest cities in the world. During Old Testament times it was also the capital of Syria. In New Testament times its ruler was controlled by the Roman emperor. Saul (Paul) became a Christian near Damascus.

damnation. Being found wrong or guilty.

damsel. Young girl (Mark 5:39).

Dan (dan). **1.** Fifth son of Jacob, and founder of one of the twelve tribes of Israel. **2.** One of the smaller tribes of Israel. Danites tried to settle an area northwest of Jerusalem, but had little success (Judges 1:34–35). At last they gave up and migrated far to the north (Judges 18), where they founded the city of Dan. **3.** City near the source of the Jordan River. It marked the northern limit of Israelite territory: "from Dan to Beer-sheba." The village of Dan is on Israel's northern border today.

Daniel (dan′yəl). **1.** Young Jew who was taken prisoner and trained for service in the Babylonian royal court (Daniel 1). Throughout his long life he bravely refused—no matter what the cost—to turn against right living and worship of the true God. He was honored by many kings and held several places of great responsibility. **2.** Old Testament book, placed fifth in the section called Major Prophets, but placed by the Hebrews themselves in a section called Writings.

Darius (də rī′əs). **1.** Darius I, great Persian king mentioned in Ezra, Nehemiah, and Haggai. **2.** Darius the Mede, mentioned in Daniel—a king about whom no one knows exact historical facts.

darkness. Besides the usual meanings, often means that which is wrong, bad, or displeasing to God (1 John 2:11); see its opposite, **light.**

David (dā′vid). Second king of Israel, who reigned about 1000–960 B.C. While still a shepherd boy, he was anointed as future king by Samuel (1 Samuel 16). King Saul came to know him as a skilful musician and a brave giant-killer. Then Saul became jealous, and David had to run for his life. He became a sort of Robin Hood, gathering a group of outlaw followers. When Saul died during a wartime defeat, David was crowned king in Hebron. Soon Saul's weak son was also killed, and David became king of the entire country. He conquered Jerusalem and made it his new capital. David is remembered as the best king Israel ever had. He is also remembered as the writer of many psalms and songs.

day. Often used to mean a future time when God will perform some mighty act. In the Old Testament it means a time when God will judge wicked people and reward righteous ones (Malachi 3:16–18; 4:5–6). In the New Testament it means a time when Christ will return (2 Thessalonians 2:1–2).

deacon. Special helper—literally, "servant"—of a church. Some people think that Acts 6:1–6 tells about the first deacons, although the word is not used.

Dead Sea. Salt lake into which the Jordan River flows. It is 53 miles long and 10 miles wide. Its water —25 per cent solid—is the densest known, and its surface is the lowest-lying spot on earth—1,292 feet below sea level. Its depths go down twice that far. No plant or animal life can live in its oily, salty waters. It is nearly always called "Salt Sea" in the Bible. Its northern half is in Jordan today; its southern half, between Jordan and Israel.

Dead Sea Scrolls (ded' sē' skrōlz'). Writings found near the Dead Sea in 1947. They tell much about the periods just before, during, and after Jesus' earthly life. The scrolls include some of the oldest known copies of Old Testament books.

deal with. To act or behave toward (Luke 2:48).

dearth. Scarcity, especially of food.

Deborah (deb'ə rə). Woman judge and prophetess who aroused the people of Israel, led by Barak, to win a great victory (Judges 4–5).

debtor. Often means a person who owes something other than money. "Our debtors" in the Lord's Prayer (Matthew 6:12) are those who owe us apologies for sinning against us. Paul was "debtor" to many people, because he owed them an opportunity to hear about Christ (Romans 1:14).

Decalogue (dek'ə lôg). Same as **Ten Commandments.**

Decapolis (də kap'ə ləs). "Ten Towns" of New Testament times that co-operated with one another as allies. Most of them lay east of the Jordan River.

decree. Official order.

dedicate. To set aside for a special purpose, especially for some religious purpose.

Dedication, Feast of (fēst' əv ded ə-kā'shən). Jewish holiday celebrating the rededication of the Temple under the leadership of Judas Maccabaeus in 165 B.C. It comes in early December (John 10:22), and is known today as **Hanukkah.**

deep, the. Ocean or other great body of water.

defile. To make unclean or tabooed; see **clean.**

degrees, song of. Same as "ascents, song of."

Delilah (də lī'lə). Woman who tricked Samson, the mighty Hebrew hero, and turned him over to his enemies, the Philistines.

deliver. Verb with several meanings, three of which are shown (in this order) in 2 Kings 18:23,30: **1.** To give. **2.** To rescue or set free. **3.** To transfer or allow another to take.

Demetrius (də mē'tri əs). Silversmith in Ephesus who led a riot against Paul. (Acts 19:24–41.)

demon. Evil spirit or **devil,** especially one that troubles a person's mind.

denarius of Caesar Augustus

denarius. Roman silver coin (sometimes translated **penny** [singular] or **pence** [plural], or simply **piece of silver**); one day's pay for a laborer in Jesus' time.

deny. 1. To say, "I do not know or believe" (Matthew 10:33). **2.** To say, "I am not concerned about" (Matthew 16:24).

deputy. In the book of Acts, same as **proconsul.**

Derbe (dûr'bi). City of Galatia (now in south central Turkey) where **Paul** preached (Acts 14:6, 20; 16:1).

deride. To make fun of.

descend. To go or come down.

descent. 1. Downward slope (Luke 19:37). **2.** Family from which one comes (Hebrews 7:3).

desire. To want or ask.

desolate. Lonely; deserted; not lived in.

despitefully (di spīt'fool i). Cruelly; hatefully (Luke 6:28).

destitute. Lacking everything; in great need.

Deuteronomy (dōō'tər än' ə mi *or* dyōō'tər än'ə mi). Fifth book of the Old Testament, and of the section known as Law. The name means "a second giving of the Law," because the book tells of a second time that Moses announced and explained laws to the Israelites, just before they entered the Promised Land. There are many opinions as to when Deuteronomy was put into writing, and by whom; but everyone agrees on the value of such great teachings as those in Deuteronomy 6:4–7.

devil. Supernatural being who tries to block God's purposes, tempt people to sin, and accuse people before God; see **Satan.** (He is also called **Beelzebub,** the **evil one,** and **Lucifer.** Sometimes the word "devil" means a chief **demon** who directs the work of other demons.

devoted. Set aside to be destroyed (Leviticus 27:28).

devout. Religious; reverent; sincere in worship.

Diana of the Ephesians (dī an'ə əv thə i fē'zhənz). Same as **Artemis of the Ephesians.**

didst. Old form of "did," used with "thou."

Didymus (did'ə məs). "Twin"; another name for **Thomas,** Jesus' disciple (John 11:16).

die (dī). Sometimes used as a figure of speech for giving up one's own way of life and living entirely for God (1 Corinthians 15:31).

diligent. Hard-working; quick to get things done in the proper way.

Dinah (dī'nə). Daughter of Jacob.

discern (di zūrn' *or* di sūrn'). **1.** To recognize (Genesis 27:23; 1 Corinthians 11:29). **2.** To tell the difference (Jonah 4:11).

disciple. Learner or pupil; one who chooses to follow a teacher or teaching. The word is used to describe Jesus' twelve closest friends, but also his other followers, and the followers of other teachers as well.

disciple whom Jesus loved. Same as **beloved disciple.**

discomfit. To trouble, weaken, upset, or defeat.

discover. 1. To uncover (Psalm 18:15). **2.** To see or recognize (Acts 21:3).

dishonor, dishonour. To bring shame upon.

dispensation. Controlling or managing of affairs.

dispersion. Scattering; usually means (especially when capitalized) the scattering of Jews into many lands during and after their exile in Assyria and Babylonia.

disputation. Argument (Romans 14:1).

dissemble. To pretend to show a feeling that you do not really have.

dissimulation. Act of **dissembling.**

distaff (dis'taf). Stick from which fibers of flax or wool are pulled as they are spun into thread on a **spindle.**

distribute. To give out or share; especially, to share with needy people (1 Timothy 6:18).

divers. Several; various; of different kinds (Mark 1:34).

divide. 1. To separate into parts (Daniel 5:28). **2.** To know and explain (2 Timothy 2:15).

divine. 1. Having to do with God (used only in Hebrews 9:1 and 2 Peter 1:3–4). **2.** Someone who has learned much about God (used in some translations as part of the title of Revelation). **3.** To learn through some religious or magic act what the future holds, or what one should do (Genesis 44:5,15).

doctor. Expert and teacher of Jewish law (Luke 2:46).

doctrine. Teaching.

doest. Old form of "do," used with "thou."

dog. Dogs as pets (Matthew 15:27) and as sheep watchers (Job 30:1) are rarely mentioned in the Bible. Most dogs were mongrels that fought for garbage in the streets. Thus it was even more of an insult in Bible times than it is today to call someone a dog (Psalm 22:16).

dominion. Power to rule or control.

Dorcas (dôr′kəs). Woman disciple who lived in Joppa and did many good works in Jesus' name. When she died, Peter brought her back to life (Acts 9:36–42).

dost. Old form of "do," used with "thou."

doth. Old form of "does," used with "he," "she," or "it."

Dothan (dō′thən). City about 45 miles north of Jerusalem; now in Jordan. There Joseph was sold as a slave by his brothers. There Elisha lived, and miraculously escaped capture by Syrian armies. The ruins of Dothan are today called Tell Dotha.

doxology. Hymn of praise to God, such as Psalm 150.

do you to wit. Let you know (2 Corinthians 8:1).

dragon. In the Old Testament, often means jackal; also serpent or sea monster.

draught. 1. Catch of fish (Luke 5:4). **2.** Is evacuated (Mark 7:19).

drink offering. Wine poured on an altar along with other sacrifices.

drought. Long period of dry weather, with little or no rain.

Drusilla (dro͞o sil′ə). Jewish princess and wife of Felix, Roman governor who heard Paul's defense (Acts 24:24).

dulcimer. Word coming at the end of a list of musical instruments named in Daniel 3:5,10,15, meaning that all the instruments were played together; not the instrument known today as a dulcimer.

dumb. Unable to speak.

dung. Manure.

dunghill. Where manure was piled for use as fertilizer.

dure. To endure (Matthew 13:21).

durst. Old past tense of "to dare" (Acts 7:32).

dwell. To stay; live; make one's home.

distaff with spindle

ear. Often used as a figure of speech for hearing or listening.

earing. Plowing (Genesis 45:6).

early rain. Autumn showers that softened the soil for early spring plowing (James 5:7); same as **former rain.**

earnest. Guarantee; down payment (Ephesians 1:14).

earthen. Clay.

east wind. Hot, dry, dusty wind from the desert; sirocco; not just any wind from the east (Genesis 41:6; Isaiah 27:8).

Easter (ēs'tər). Sunday in early spring when Christians especially remember Jesus' resurrection. It is not really a Bible word; its one use in some versions (Acts 12:4) should be translated **Passover.**

Ebal (ē'bəl). Bare, rocky mountain in Samaria that forms one side of an important pass; now Jabal 'Aybāl in northwestern Jordan.

Ebed-melech (ē'bid mel'ik). Ethiopian court official in Jerusalem who saved Jeremiah from death (Jeremiah 38).

Ecclesiastes (i klē'zi as'tēz). Old Testament book, usually classified as Poetry, and as one of the Writings in the Hebrew Bible. Some people think the writer was Solomon, but he never plainly says so. The book perhaps asks more questions than it answers—about God's ways with men, about what is right for men to do, about how men can know what to do. The writer urges that people honor and obey God, starting to do so while they are still young.

Eden (ē'd'n). Garden where Adam and Eve lived (Genesis 2–3).

edict. Official order.

edify. To build up; to strengthen (Acts 9:31).

Edom (ē'dəm), **Edomites** (ē'də mīts'). Nation descended from Esau. They lived in the rocky area south of the Dead Sea (now in Jordan), and were usually enemies of their relatives, the Hebrews.

Egypt (ē'jipt), **Egyptians** (i jip'shəns). One of the oldest nations in the world (now officially included in the United Arab Republic), and one of the greatest in early times. Jacob's sons came to the fertile Nile valley to buy food when their own area was dry and barren. Later, their descendants became slaves of the Egyptians, but were set free in the time of Moses. Egypt invaded Israel and Judah more than once in later centuries, but became less and less powerful. In New Testament times Egypt belonged to Rome.

Elath, Eloth (ē'ləth). Same as **Eziongaber** or **Ezion-geber.**

elder. Older leader in a family, tribe, or religious group—either one living now, or one whose past words or deeds are remembered; same as **presbyter.**

elect. Person or persons chosen by God for a special purpose.

Eli (ē'lī). Old priest at Shiloh who taught the boy Samuel and was helped by him (1 Samuel 1–4).

Eli, Eli, lama sabach-thani (ē'lī ē'lī lä'mə sə bak'thə nī). Same as **"Eloi, Eloi, lama sabach-thani."**

Eliezer (el'i ē'zər). Name of several Old Testament characters; one of them was Abraham's servant (Genesis 15:2)—probably the same servant who was sent to get a wife for Isaac (Genesis 24).

Elijah (i lī'jə), **Elias** (i lī'əs). Great prophet of Israel, the Northern Kingdom, about 875–850 B.C. Elijah dared to stand alone for the Lord God, even when he had to tell kings that they had done wrong. His victory over the priests of Baal on Mount Carmel makes one of the most thrilling stories in the Bible (1 Kings 18).

Elisabeth (i liz'ə bəth). Same as **Elizabeth.**

36

Elisha (i lī'shə). **Eliseus** (el'ə sē'əs). Great prophet of Israel, the Northern Kingdom, about 850–800 B.C. Elisha was Elijah's disciple and successor (1 Kings 19:19). He performed miracles of helpfulness and advised kings about God's will.

Elizabeth (i liz'ə bəth). Wife of Zacharias, mother of John the Baptist, and relative of Mary, Jesus' mother (Luke 1); same as **Elisabeth.**

Elkanah (el kā'nə). Father of Samuel (1 Samuel 1).

Eloi, Eloi, lama sabach-thani (ē'lō ī ē'lō ī lä'mə sə bak'thə nī). My God, my God, why hast thou forsaken me? (An **Aramaic** quotation from Psalm 22:1, spoken by Jesus on the cross; same as **"Eli, Eli, lama sabach-thani."**)

Elul (ē'lul). Sixth month of the Hebrew year—August-September.

Emmanuel (i man'yoo el). Same as **Immanuel.**

Emmaus (e mā'əs). Judean town 7-1/2 miles from Jerusalem, to which Jesus walked with two disciples on the day of his resurrection. Four present-day towns in Israel and Jordan all claim to be Emmaus.

En-gedi (en ged'ī). Oasis about the middle of the western shore of the Dead Sea. Near here David hid from jealous King Saul. The modern Israeli town is called Ein Gedi.

enmity. Opposition; fighting; hatred.

Enoch (ē'nək). Man in ancient times who lived so close to God that at last "he was not, for God took him" (Genesis 5:24).

ensample (en sam'p'l). Example.

entreat. (Same as **intreat.**) **1.** To beg or plead (Philippians 4:3). **2.** To treat (Luke 20:11).

Epaphras (ep'ə frəs *or* i paf'rəs). Christian leader in Colossae and nearby cities who was Paul's fellow prisoner in Rome.

Epaphroditus (i paf'rə dī'təs). Christian leader in Philippi who took his church's gift to Paul in prison at Rome and returned with the letter that we call Philippians.

ephah. Dry measure—about 3/8 to 2/3 of a bushel.

Ephesians (i fē'zhənz). Letter written by Paul to the church at Ephesus (and perhaps to other churches as well). Placed fifth in the section of the New Testament called Paul's Letters, it expresses some of the greatest and highest ideas ever written about God and his plan for the world. It also urges Christians to be good church members, good family members, and faithful soldiers for Christ.

Ephesus (ef'ə səs). Great seaport city in the Roman province of Asia (now western Turkey). Here Paul preached for three years. He made so many converts that those who worshiped a pagan goddess, Artemis of the Ephesians, got worried and started a riot. Ephesus became one of the strongest centers of early Christianity. Today the ruins of the city lie 4 or 5 miles from the sea.

ephod (ē'fäd). Short smock worn by priests and sometimes by others.

high priest's ephod

37

It was made sometimes of white linen, sometimes of many colors, sometimes with golden outer layers.

ephphatha (ef'ə thə). Be opened! (**Aramaic** word used by Jesus—Mark 7:34.)

Ephraim (ē'fri əm). **1.** Second son of Joseph and an Egyptian mother. He was "adopted" by his grandfather Jacob and counted as the forefather of one of the twelve tribes (Genesis 48). **2.** Tribe of Israel that settled a strip of land stretching northward from Jericho and westward to the Mediterranean (Joshua 16:5). **3.** Name for Israel, the Northern Kingdom, during the later part of its history. It was so called because it had lost much of its land, and the territory of the tribe of Ephraim was almost all it had left (Hosea 5:3). **4.** Forest east of the Jordan River (2 Samuel 18:6). **5.** Town north of Jerusalem (John 11:54).

Ephratah (ef'rə tä), **Ephrath** (ef'rəth), **Ephrathah** (ef'rə thə). Same as **Bethlehem.**

epistle. Letter, especially a letter that has become a book in the New Testament.

ere. Before.

err. To do wrong or be wrong; to make a mistake.

Esaias (e zā'əs). Same as **Isaiah.**

Esau (ē'sô). Son of Isaac and Rebekah; elder twin brother of Jacob. He traded away his birthright, and was cheated out of his father's special blessing (Genesis 25:29–34). He and Jacob were enemies for years, but later became friendly again.

eschew. To stay away from; avoid; shun.

Eshbaal (esh'bāl). Same as **Ish-bosheth.**

espoused (i spouzd'). Engaged to be married with such firm agreement that only a divorce could break it.

Essenes (es'ēnz). Strict religious group of Jews in Jesus' day; not mentioned in the Bible. The Dead Sea Scrolls once belonged to an Essene community.

estate. 1. Place (Daniel 11:20–21). **2.** Condition (Luke 1:48).

esteem. To consider; to think of.

Esther (es'tər or es'thər). **1.** Beautiful Jewish girl (also called **Hadassah**) among the exiles who had been carried away into Babylonia. Persia had now defeated Babylonia, and Esther became the new queen of a Persian ruler. With the help of her wise cousin Mordecai, she discovered a wicked plot and saved her fellow Jews from death. **2.** Old Testament book that tells the story of Esther. The Jews called it one of the Writings; today it is placed last in the History section.

eternal. Lasting forever; never changing.

Ethiopia (ē'thi ō'piə). **Ethiopians** (ē'-thi ō'pi əns). Nation in eastern Africa that is one of the oldest in the world. In Bible times dark-skinned Ethiopians lived in what is now Sudan. Ebed-melech, who rescued Jeremiah (Jeremiah 38:7), and the queen's treasurer, whom Philip told about Jesus (Acts 8:27), were both Ethiopians.

Eunice (yōō'nis). Timothy's mother (2 Timothy 1:5).

eunuch (yōō'nək). Man who is physically unable to become a father (Daniel 1:3; Acts 8:27). Eunuchs were often court officials in Old Testament times.

Euphrates (yoo frā'tēz). Greatest river of western Asia, often called in the Bible simply "the **river**" (Isaiah 7:20). Today called Firat in Turkey, Al Furāt in Syria, it flows through both countries, and on through Iraq and along the border of Iran into the Persian Gulf.

Euroclydon (yoo rə klī'dən). Strong, dangerous wind; northeaster.

Eutychus (yōō'tə kəs). Young man in Troas who went to sleep during an all-night sermon by Paul and fell from his perch in a third-floor window. Paul brought him back to life.

evangelist. 1. Someone who tells the good news about Jesus (Acts 21:8). **2.** The writer of any one of the four Gospels.

Eve (ēv). First woman told about in the Bible; Adam's wife. First she, then Adam disobeyed God and so could no longer live the kind of life God had planned for them (Genesis 2–5).

even. 1. Evening (Mark 1:32). **2.** Exactly; just (Luke 19:32). **3** .Though it may seem unlikely; indeed (Luke 12:7). **4.** Flat; smooth (Psalm 26: 12).

everlasting. Never ending.

evil. Wrong; bad.

evil one, the. Satan; the **devil.**

evil spirit. Same as **demon.**

exalt. 1. To worship or praise (Psalm 99:9). **2.** To lift up or make higher in power, dignity, or rank (Luke 1:52).

exceeding. 1. Very (Matthew 2:10). **2.** Extreme; more than usual (Ephesians 1:19).

excellency. Greatness; state of being greater than others (Ecclesiastes 7:12).

except. 1. Unless (John 3:3). **2.** Other than; leaving out; but (Acts 8:1).

exhort. To encourage; to comfort (Acts 14:22).

exile. Period during which the Jews were forced to live elsewhere than their own area. Sometimes the word includes the Assyrian captivity of Israel, the Northern Kingdom, beginning between 740 and 721 B.C. Sometimes it means only the Babylonian captivity of Judah,

the Southern Kingdom, beginning between 605 and 587 B.C. The period of the Exile ended in 538 B.C.

Exodus (ek'sə dəs). **1.** Departure from Egypt by the Israelites who had been slaves. The word means going out. God's rescue of his people was ever after looked back upon as the most important event of Old Testament times. **2.** Old Testament book that tells about the Exodus from Egypt. It is placed second in the books of Law, and includes the Ten Commandments. It also includes much history—the life of Moses, the plagues in Egypt, the Exodus itself, the wanderings in the desert, the building of the tabernacle.

exorcise, exorcize. To drive out evil spirits.

expound. To explain.

extol, extoll. To praise highly.

extortion. Getting money or other property from someone by force or threats.

eyeservice. Doing what looks right, rather than what really is right (Ephesians 6:6).

Ezekiel (i zē'ki əl). **1.** Jewish prophet who was taken to Babylonia as a captive in 598 B.C. (Ezekiel 1:3). He warned his people that Jerusalem would be punished for its sins. After Jerusalem was destroyed in 587 B.C., Ezekiel changed his message to one of encouragement and hope for the future. **2.** Book containing Ezekiel's life and prophecies, placed in the Major Prophets section of the Old Testament. It includes many important teachings and beautiful poems, and had a strong effect on the writing of several books of the New Testament.

Ezion-gaber, Ezion-geber (e zi ən gē'bər *or* e zi ən gā'ber). Seaport and mining city on the northeastern tip of the Red Sea; same as **Elath** or **Eloth.** Kings of Judah had fleets and metal foundries there. Ruins of the old city are now in the south-western edge of Jordan. Across the border in Israel, a new port city uses a form of one of the old names: Eilat.

Ezra (ez′rə). **1.** Jewish priest and scribe who came back from Babylonia to Jerusalem, probably in 458 B.C. He helped to start again the pure worship of God and taught God's laws. His story is told in Ezra 7–10 and Nehemiah 8–10. **2.** Old Testament book of History. It tells about the first return of Jewish exiles from Babylonia in 538 B.C., the rebuilding of the Temple in Jerusalem, and the beginning of Ezra's work.

F

fain. Gladly (Luke 15:16).

Fair Havens (fer hā′vənz *or* far hä′-vəns). Inadequate harbor on the southern coast of Crete where Paul's ship stopped briefly (Acts 27:8–13); still known today by the Greek words for "Fair Havens."

faith. 1. Belief in something or trust in some person; especially, trust in God or Christ. It involves not only a first decision to trust, but also a continuing attitude of trust throughout life (Ephesians 2:8). **2.** True religion; usually "the faith" (Acts 16:5; Jude 3).

Fall, the. Coming of sin into the world, especially as described in the Genesis story of Adam and Eve. The Bible does not use this exact phrase, but often speaks of people falling into sin (1 Timothy 6:9).

false witness. Untrue report; lie.

familiar spirit. Spirit of a dead person that was supposed to tell secrets through the words of a medium or wizard.

famine. Great lack of food; time of starvation.

fan (pitchfork)

fan. Pitchfork, used to throw grain into the air so that the chaff can be blown away (Luke 3:17).

farthing showing shields and palm tree

farthing. One of the smallest Roman copper coins; 1/10 to 1/40 of a denarius.

fashion. 1. To form or shape (Psalm 119:73). **2.** Appearance or likeness (Luke 9:29).

fast. 1. To go without food, because of sadness, sorrow for sin, or desire to think about holy things instead of earthly things (Nehemiah 1:4). **2.** Day or period of fasting (Jonah 3:5). **3.** Fastened tight; steady (Judges 16:11). **4.** Speedily (Ezra 5:8).

fat. Often means, not overweight, but having so many earthly possessions that one forgets God (Nehemiah 9:25).

father. 1. Male parent (Exodus 20: 12). **2.** Name for God (usually capitalized—Romans 1:7). **3.** Any ancestor (Genesis 48:15). **4.** Title of honor (1 Samuel 24:11). **5.** Someone important to the beginning of something; founder (Genesis 4:20).

fathom. Unit for measuring depth of water—from fingertips to fingertips with arms outstretched, or about 6 feet.

favor, favour. 1. To like, approve, or help (Psalm 41:11). **2.** Liking or approval (Luke 2:52).

fear. Fearing God means much more than being afraid of his power. It also includes respecting him, recognizing that he is great and holy, worshiping him, and trying to do his will (Psalm 111:10).

feast. 1. Great dinner or banquet (Luke 5:29). **2.** Great religious celebration; festival (John 13:1).

feign. To pretend or lie.

Felix (fē'liks). Roman governor of Judea before whom Paul had his first trial in Caesarea (Acts 23–24). He kept Paul in prison, hoping for a bribe.

fenced city. Walled, fortified city or town; see **village.**

fervent. Having warm or strong feeling.

festal garment. Man's robe for special occasions (Genesis 45:22 in some translations).

Festus (fes'təs). Roman governor of Judea who succeeded Felix and conducted Paul's second trial in Caesarea. He sent Paul on to the emperor in Rome (Acts 24–25).

fetters. Foot chains.

figure. 1. Form, shape, or outline (Deuteronomy 4:16). **2.** Something that means more than it seems to; something that stands for, or reminds one of, something else (Romans 5:14).

fine. To refine (Job 28:1).

finger of God. Often used as a figure of speech for the power of God (Exodus 8:19).

firkin. Liquid measure; about 10 gallons (John 2:6).

firmament. Sky.

firstborn, first-born. Hebrews believed that the oldest offspring of man or animal belonged in a special way to God. Firstborn animals were sacrificed; other animals usually were substituted as sacrifices for firstborn sons. A firstborn son had the birthright and a special blessing from his father.

firstfruits. First part of the harvest, made a **sacrifice** as a sign that all of the harvest comes from God. The phrase is used as a figure of speech in the New Testament (1 Corinthians 15:20).

flag. Marsh grass (Exodus 2:3).

flagon. 1. Large wine pitcher (Isaiah 22:24). **2.** In some verses, the word should be translated "cake of raisins" (2 Samuel 6:19).

flesh. Often used as a figure of speech for one's whole body (2 John 7); all mankind (Matthew 16:17); all living beings (Psalm 136:25); one's relatives (Genesis 2:23–24); or the physical part of one's nature (Romans 8:9).

flood. 1. Any overflowing stream (Joshua 24:15). **2.** Great overflow described in Genesis 6–9.

floor. 1. Bottom surface (1 Kings 6:15). **2.** Place where grain was **threshed** and **winnowed** (Joel 2:24).

prisoner in fetters

41

fold. 1. Sheep pen (John 10:16). **2.** Number of times or number of parts (Mark 4:20).

folly. Foolishness.

forasmuch as. Since.

forbear. 1. To hold back or keep from (Ezekiel 24:17). **2.** To put up with; to show self-control (Ephesians 4:2).

forerunner. John the Baptist—so called because he came before Jesus did, to prepare the way.

forgive. To excuse or pardon; to give up angry feelings or desire to punish.

former rain. Same as **early rain.**

fornication. Adultery and other similar sins.

forsake. To give up; to go away from; to leave.

forsomuch as. Since.

forswear. To swear to something untrue.

forth. Out; into view.

for that. Because (Romans 5:12).

forthwith. At once.

fowl. Bird or birds.

frankincense branch

frankincense. Chunks of dried, whitish resin from certain trees; when ground into powder and burned, it gives a spicy smell. Frankincense

was used in the Temple, and was one of the Wise Men's gifts.

Freedmen (frēd'mən). Jews who were freed Roman captives or children of such captives; same as **Libertines** (Acts 6:9). Probably because they spoke Greek, they had a special synagogue in Jerusalem.

frontlet

frontlets. Objects tied onto the forehead during prayer; one type of **phylacteries.**

froward. Stubborn; contrary; perverse.

fruit. Often means the result or product of some action or disposition (Galatians 5:22).

fulfil. To carry out; make to happen; complete.

fuller. Man who bleaches cloth by washing it with a special soap and spreading it to dry in a "fullers' field" outside a city (Isaiah 7:3; Malachi 3:2; Mark 9:3).

furlong. Measure of distance; 1/8 of a mile; same as **stadion.**

G

Gabriel (gā'bri əl). One of God's angels who takes messages to people on earth (Luke 1:19,26).

Gad (gad). **1.** Seventh son of Jacob (Genesis 30:11). **2.** Tribe of Israel

(Numbers 32:31). **3.** Prophet who helped King David (1 Samuel 22:5).

Gadara (gad′ə rə), **Gadarenes** (gad′ə-rēnz). City of the Decapolis, southeast of the Sea of Galilee (now in Jordan). This may have been the home of a man whose mind Jesus healed (Matthew 8:28).

gainsay. To contradict.

Galatia (gə lā′shə). Roman province whose inhabitants were descended from the Gauls that settled in France. The area is now in central Turkey; Ancyra, capital of Galatia, is now Ankara, capital of Turkey. Paul started churches in some of the Galatian cities.

Galatians (gə lā′shənz). New Testament book; one of Paul's letters, written probably to the churches he started in cities of Galatia, but possibly to other churches in the province. Some people were claiming that Paul was not really an apostle of Jesus Christ. Some were saying that Christians must obey all the Jewish laws, and some that Christians need not obey any laws at all. To meet all of these false ideas, Paul wrote some of his strongest and fieriest words.

Galilee (gal′ə lē). Area between the Sea of Galilee (and the Jordan River just north and south of it) and the Mediterranean Sea. This was the northernmost part of Israel, the Northern Kingdom. In New Testament times Galilee was a Roman province. The entire area is now in Israel. Galilee is most famous as the scene of much of Jesus' life and work.

Galilee, Sea of (sē′ əv gal′ə lē). Freshwater lake formed by the Jordan River and other streams. It has had many other names: **Chinnereth, Chinneroth, Gennesaret, Tiberias.** Today Israelis call it Kinneret; Arabs call it Tabariyeh. The entire lake is in Israel, although for several miles only a 33-foot strip of beach separates it from Syria. Galilee is heart-shaped—13 miles long, and 8 miles wide at its widest point. Its blue-green waters go as deep as 200 feet and contain many fish. Sudden, dangerous storms are caused by cold winds blowing down steep mountains nearby.

gall. Bitter, poisonous herb, and the juice of that herb.

Gamaliel (gə mā′li əl). Famous Hebrew scribe and teacher; the apostle Paul was his best-known pupil.

garment. Piece of clothing.

garner. Storehouse for grain.

garnish. To decorate (Revelation 21:

43

19); to arrange or set in order (Luke 11:25).

Gath (gath). One of the Philistines' great cities, about halfway between Jerusalem and Gaza (near the seacoast). Giants such as Goliath lived in Gath. No one knows exactly where in modern Israel the ruins of Gath lie.

Gath-hepher (gath hē'fər). Galilean hometown of Jonah, probably about 3 miles northeast of Nazareth (now in northern Israel).

Gaza (gā'zə *or* gä'zə). One of the Philistines' great cities, southwest of Jerusalem, near the seacoast. It lies on important roads, and was the greatest trade center of the whole area in Bible times. Today Gaza and the strip of land surrounding it is a no-man's-land—crammed with Arab refugees and controlled by Egypt.

Gehazi (gi hā'zī). Servant of the prophet Elisha (2 Kings 4:12).

Gehenna (gi hen'ə). Name for **hell,** definition **2.**

gender (jen'dər). To give birth to (2 Timothy 2:23).

General Epistles. Same as **General Letters.**

General Letters. Section of New Testament books including Hebrews, James, 1 and 2 Peter, 1 and 2 and 3 John, and Jude. They are also called **General Epistles.** Both of these names mean that most of the letters were written to Christians in general, or at least to Christians in several different churches, rather than to individual Christians or churches.

generation. 1. All the people who are living at about the same time (Exodus 1:6; Luke 7:31). **2.** Descendants; family line or family tree ("generations"—Genesis 6:9).

Genesis (jen'ə sis). First book in the Bible and in the Old Testament section called Law. Its first 11 chapters

tell about the beginning of all things. (The very word "Genesis" means beginning.) Genesis covers a greater length of time than any other Bible book. It tells that God made all things, including man, and that man disobeyed God. It includes many of the most familiar (and most important) Old Testament stories.

Gennesaret (ge nes'ə rət). Same as **"Galilee, Sea of"** (Luke 5:1).

Gentiles (jen'tīlz). People who are not Jews; foreign nations.

Gerasa (ger'ə sə). **1.** Important Roman city east of the Jordan River and southeast of the Sea of Galilee. It was a city of the **Decapolis,** and is now known as Jarash (in Jordan). **2.** Town on the eastern shore of the Sea of Galilee which may have been the home of a man whose mind Jesus healed (Mark 5:1).

Gergesa (ger'gə sə). Possibly the same as **Gerasa,** definition **2.**

Gerizim (ger'ə zim). Mountain in Samaria, which (with Mount Ebal) guards an important pass and crossroads (now in northwestern Jordan). The Samaritans worshiped God there (John 4:20–21), and their descendants still do so today.

Gethsemane (geth sem'ə ni). Olive orchard east of Jerusalem (on or near the Mount of Olives) where Jesus prayed in agony just before Judas led his enemies to the spot.

Gibeah (gib'i ə). City on a hilltop 3-1/2 miles north of Jerusalem (now in Jordan). It was Saul's hometown and the first royal capital of Israel. Sometimes it is called "Gibeah of Benjamin" or "Gibeah of Saul" because other places had similar names.

Gibeon (gib'i ən). City 6 miles northwest of Jerusalem. Its inhabitants tricked Joshua into protecting rather than fighting them (Joshua 9–

10). At one time Gibeon was an important center of worship; there King Solomon sacrificed and had the famous dream in which he chose wisdom. The Jordanian town is now called Al Jīb.

Gideon (gid'i ən). One of the more important leaders of Israel during the time of the judges; also called **Jerubbaal.** He defeated the Midianite desert raiders with only 300 men, but refused to start a kingdom (Judges 6–8.)

Gilboa (gil bō'ə). Mountain southwest of the Sea of Galilee where King Saul and his son Jonathan died fighting the Philistines; now on the Israeli border.

Gilead (gil'i əd). Mountainous area east of the Jordan River and southeast of the Sea of Galilee. It was

gird. **1.** To put a piece of clothing around, as a belt (John 13:4). **2.** To fasten with a belt (Psalm 45:3). **3.** To strengthen; to get ready for action (Psalm 18:32).

girdle. A long piece of leather or cloth, worn around the waist. Slits in the girdle provided pockets for carrying knives, coins, inkhorns, and food (2 Kings 1:8; 1 Samuel 18:4; Matthew 3:4).

Girgashites (gūr' gə shīts). Canaanite tribe driven out by the Israelites.

girt. Past participle of **gird** (Ephesians 6:14).

give place. To give an opportunity (Ephesians 4:27).

give up the ghost. To die.

glass. Mirror—actually made of metal in Bible times (1 Corinthians 13:12).

gleaners in a grain field

often a battleground. David escaped into this area from his rebellious son Absalom. Today Gilead is in Jordan.

Gilgal (gil'gal). **1.** City somewhere near Jericho (now in Jordan) that became Joshua's headquarters. From here the Israelites marched out to conquer other cities of Canaan. **2.** City about 7 miles north of Bethel (now in Jordan), mentioned in stories about Elijah and Elisha (2 Kings 2:1).

glean. To gather grain left in the field after the harvesters are through (Ruth 2).

glorify. **1.** To praise and worship (Psalm 86:9). **2.** To give glory to; to make splendid (John 16:14).

glory. **1.** Fame, power, splendor (Matthew 4:8). **2.** Praise (Psalm 96:8). **3.** To be proud and happy (Psalm 105:3). **4.** To boast (Galatians 6:14).

gluttonous. Greedy for food; hoggish.

goad (gōd). Pointed stick, sometimes

tipped with iron, that was used in driving and guiding animals; same as **pricks.**

god. Any person or thing that is worshiped (1 Corinthians 8:4–6).

God. The one true God known to people in Old Testament times as the Lord (**Yahweh** or **Jehovah**), and to Christians as the Father of our Lord Jesus Christ (1 Corinthians 8:4–6). God is also called by many other names in the Bible. Most of these names tell ways that inspired writers tried to describe his love and greatness.

God forbid. Let it not be! Far from it!

Godhead. That which is God; divinity; deity.

God speed. May God watch over you as you go!

Gog and Magog (gog′ ənd · mā′gog). Names mentioned in Ezekiel 38–39 and Revelation 20 as having something to do with the great Battle of Armageddon. No one really knows what the names mean.

Golden Rule. Jesus' command in Matthew 7:12 and Luke 6:31. The first time anyone so titled this rule was in A.D. 1674.

Golgotha (gäl′gə thə). Place outside the walls of Jerusalem where Jesus was crucified; same as **Calvary.** Both names mean skull. No one knows which (if either) of two places in Jordan shown to modern tourists was Golgotha, though one of the places is a hill that seems shaped like a skull. (No one even knows for sure, however, that Golgotha was a hill.)

Goliath (gə lī′əth). Giant Philistine warrior killed by young David (1 Samuel 17).

Gomorrah, Gomorrha (gə môr ə). City destroyed by fire. Its ruins may lie beneath the southern end of the Dead Sea.

goodly. Handsome or pleasing (Genesis 39:6).

goodman. Husband or master of the household.

gopher wood. Wood used in building Noah's ark; probably the same as cypress wood.

Goshen (gō′shən). Area of Egypt in which the Israelites lived. It was called the "best of the land," and was probably the northeastern part of the fertile Nile delta.

gospel. 1. "God-spell"—a story about or from God. However, this old English word translates a Greek word that really means good news. The two words together give a fair idea of the meaning of "gospel": good news from God, who sent Jesus Christ to be our Lord and Saviour (1 Thessalonians 2:9). **2.** One of the four major books about Jesus—Matthew, Mark, Luke, or John (usually capitalized).

go to. Expression used at the beginning of a statement, meaning "Come" or "Come now."

gourd. In Jonah 4, probably means the castor bean plant.

grace. 1. Beauty (Proverbs 1:9; James 1:11). **2.** Ability to please; favor; pleasing manner (Ruth 2:10). **3.** God's free, unearned love, shown to man in Jesus Christ (Ephesians 2:8).

gracious. 1. Graceful; well-suited (Luke 4:22). **2.** Merciful; loving; forgiving (Psalm 103:8).

graff. To graft (Romans 11).

grant. To give when asked.

graveclothes. Cloths wrapped around a body as preparation for burial (John 11:44).

graven image. Idol carved from stone, wood, or metal.

Great Commission (grāt′ kə mish′ən). Jesus' command that Christians tell the world about him; especially the command in Matthew 28:19–20.

Great Sea. Hebrew name for the Mediterranean (Numbers 34:6).

Grecia (grē'shə). Same as **Greece.**

Grecians (grē'shənz). In Old Testament, people of Greece (Joel 3:6); in New Testament, not Greeks, but Greek-speaking Jews, especially those who were born or lived outside Palestine (Acts 6:1); same as **Hellenists.**

Greece (grēs), **Greeks** (grēks). Nation in the southern part of the Balkan Peninsula, southeastern Europe; same as **Grecia.** Its greatest period was during Old Testament times, but there was little contact then between Greeks and Hebrews. Alexander the Great was a Macedonian (from north of Greece), and his favorite teacher was a Greek. He conquered Greece and most of the rest of the world known in his day, carrying Greek ideas and the Greek language everywhere he went. Even when the Roman Empire had defeated Alexander's successors and turned Greece into the province of Achaia, Greek was still the common language. Thus it happened that the New Testament was written in Greek.

grievous. Hard to bear; severe; very bad.

grind. To make flour or meal from grain by crushing it between two stones (Matthew 24:41).

grove. Same as **Asherah.**

grudge. 1. To grumble (James 5:9). **2.** Bad feeling against someone (Leviticus 19:18).

guestchamber. Hospitality was common in Bible lands. A large home might have a separate room reserved for guests (Mark 14:14). See also **upper room.**

guile. Slyness; dishonesty.

guilt offering. Same as **trespass offering.**

Habakkuk (hə bak'ək). **1.** Prophet of Judah, the Southern Kingdom, who lived about 600 B.C. Almost nothing is known about him. **2.** Old Testament book of the Minor Prophets. In the first two chapters the prophet asks God some hard questions: Why do good people suffer? Why do bad people seem to win? God's answer is that the evil inside bad people will finally destroy them, but that "the just shall live by his faith" (2:4). Chapter 3 of the little book is a beautiful prayer psalm expressing faith in God, no matter what happens.

habitation. Place in which to live.

Hadassah (hə das'sə). Same as **Esther** (Esther 2:7).

Hades (hā'dēz). Name for **hell,** definition **2.**

hadst. Old form of "had," used with "thou" (John 11:21).

Hagar (hā'gär). Sarah's Egyptian maid; mother of Ishmael.

Haggai (hag'i *or* hag'ī). **1.** Prophet who lived in Jerusalem after some of the Jews had come back from the Exile. In 520 B.C. he encouraged the people and their leaders to rebuild God's Temple. He may have been an old man at the time, who could remember the first Temple that had been destroyed in 587 B.C. **2.** One of the shortest Old Testament books of the Minor Prophets, containing four speeches Haggai made to encourage the rebuilding of the Temple.

hail. 1. Greetings! May joy come to you! (Luke 1:28.) **2.** Hailstones (Exodus 9:18).

hallelujah. Praise the Lord!

hallow. To make holy or sacred; to separate from ordinary things or people.

halt. 1. Lame or crippled (Luke 14: 21). **2.** To limp (1 Kings 18:21).

Ham (ham). Noah's youngest son.

Haman (hā′mən). Prime minister of Persia who plotted against Queen Esther and all other Jews (Esther 3–7).

Hamath (hā′math), **Hemath** (hē′math). Important city and kingdom on the Orontes River in Syria; its southern border was the northern border of Israel when at its largest size (1 Kings 8:65). Today the city is called Ḥamāh.

hand. Often used as a figure of speech for power (Psalm 71:4).

handmaid, handmaiden (hand′mād-′n). Woman servant.

handywork, or **handiwork.** Something done or made by someone (Psalm 19:1).

hanging. Curtain (Numbers 3:31).

Hannah (han′ə). Samuel's mother, who prayed to have a son, and then dedicated him to God's work (1 Samuel 1).

Hanukkah (hä′nōō kä). Same as "Dedication, Feast of."

hap. Luck; good fortune.

haply. Perhaps.

Haran (har′ən). **1.** Abraham's brother and Lot's father (Genesis 11:26–31). **2.** City in the northern Euphrates Valley (now in southeastern Turkey) where Abraham and his family moved from Ur, on their way to Canaan. Many of his relatives stayed there. People of Haran worshiped a moon god.

hard by, hard to. Close to (1 Kings 21:1; Acts 18:7).

harlot. Prostitute.

harp. One of the main musical instruments in Bible times; much the same as **lyre, psaltery,** and **viol.**

David's harp was probably a very simple one with three strings; some harps had as many as twenty. Eleven or more harps were played in the Temple.

hart. Male deer.

harvest. The gathering or **reaping** of ripe crops or fruit. In Bible times flax was harvested in March and April; barley in April and early May; wheat in May and June; figs, grapes, and pomegranates in August and September; and olives from mid-September to mid-November.

hast. Old form of "have," used with "thou."

haste. 1. To hurry (Genesis 24:18). **2.** Hurry; speed (Exodus 12:11; Luke 19:5).

hasten. To hurry.

hath. Old form of "has," used with "he," "she," "it."

haughty. Too proud (Psalm 131:1).

haven. Harbor (Acts 27:12).

Hazor (hā′zôr). Important city 10 miles north of the Sea of Galilee. Scene of great battles won by Joshua, Deborah, and Barak. Today its ruins lie in northern Israel.

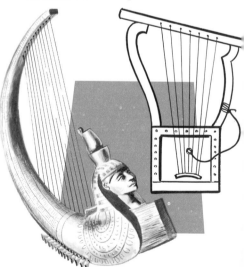

Egyptian harp and Hebrew lyre

48

harvesting grain

heady. Reckless (2 Timothy 3:4).

hearken. To listen carefully; to pay attention.

heart. Often used as a figure of speech, meaning not only a person's inner feelings but also his thoughts and mental powers. Hebrews sometimes said "heart" when people of today would say "mind" or "brain" or "head" (1 Kings 3:9,12).

heathen. People who are not Jews (Galatians 2:9) and do not know the true God (Matthew 6:7).

heaven. 1. Sky as seen from the earth; place from which sunshine and rain come; space through which move the sun, stars, moon, and so on (Genesis 22:17). **2.** Where God, Christ, and angels are believed to be in some special sense (Matthew 6:9); no one knows exactly what or where "heaven" is (in this meaning). **3.** Word used in place of the word "God" (Matthew 10:7). See also **Paradise.**

heaviness. Sadness (Proverbs 10:1).

Hebrew (hē′brōō). **1.** Abraham or one of his descendants; same as Israelite or Jew (Genesis 14:13; Philippians 3:5). **2.** Language in which nearly all of the Old Testament was written. (See **Aramaic** for the few exceptions.) It is written from right to left with an alphabet of 22 letters. Use of many picture words makes Hebrew a colorful and down-to-earth language.

Hebrews (hē′brōōz). New Testament book; first in the section called General Letters, though very little about it makes it seem like a letter. Actually, it is a sermon or essay. It was written to help Jews understand that Jesus is the Messiah whom God promised to send. One of the most famous passages is the "Roll Call of Heroes of Faith" in 11:1 to 12:2. No one knows who wrote Hebrews; many New Testament Christians have been suggested as the writer. God inspired it, and this is what really matters.

Hebron (hē′brən). City 19 miles southwest of Jerusalem (now in

Jordan). Abraham lived there (see **Mamre**) and was buried nearby (see **Mach-pelah**). It was David's first capital, before he became king of the entire country.

heed. Careful attention.

hell. 1. Place where dead people are, often thought of as being under the earth (Psalm 139:8); sometimes called **Sheol** or the **pit. 2.** Place where wicked or unbelieving people go after death (Luke 16:23); sometimes called **Hades** or **Gehenna.**

Hellenists (hel'ə nists). Same as **Grecians.**

Roman helmet

helmet. Headgear worn in battle to protect the head.

hence. Away from here (John 2:16); away from now (Acts 1:5).

henceforth, henceforward. From now on.

herb. Often means any green plant, not just those called herbs today (Genesis 1:29–30).

hereafter. After this; from now on.

hereby. By this.

herein. In this.

hereof. Of this.

heresy. False religious belief.

heretic. Person who believes **heresy.**

heretofore. Before now; up to now.

hereunto. For this.

herewith. With this.

Hermes (hūr'mēz). Messenger for the gods in Greek mythology; simi-lar to **Mercurius** or Mercury (Acts 14:12).

Hermon (hūr'mən). Mountain west of Damascus and northeast of the Sea of Galilee (now on the Syrian-Lebanese border). Its nine-thousand-foot peak can be seen at great distances. Some people think that Jesus' transfiguration took place here.

Herod (her'əd). **1.** Family name of Judean kings in New Testament times. **2.** King Herod the Great, ruler when Jesus was born (Matthew 2). He talked with the Wise Men and tried to have Jesus killed. **3.** Herod Antipas, son of Herod the Great, who ruled part of his father's former kingdom (Luke 9:7). He had John the Baptist beheaded and held one of Jesus' trials. **4.** Herod Agrippa I, grandson of Herod the Great, who ruled over most of his grandfather's former kingdom (Acts 12:1,6). He had James the apostle killed and planned to execute Peter.

Herodians (hi rō'di ənz). Jews who wanted their country freed from the Romans and ruled by one of the Herods.

Herodias (hi rō'di əs). Granddaughter of Herod the Great who married her own uncle, then divorced him to marry Herod Antipas, another uncle. She and her daughter Salome helped to cause the death of John the Baptist (Mark 6:16–29).

hew. To cut.

Hezekiah (hez'ə kī'ə). King of Judah, the Southern Kingdom, about 715–686 B.C. (2 Kings 18). He was one of the better kings, and tried to lead his people back to God.

Hiddekel (hid'ə kəl). Same as **Tigris** (Daniel 10:4).

high place. Hilltop altar—sometimes for worship of the true God, sometimes for worship of others.

high priest. Highest religious position among the Hebrews; same as **chief priest.** The high priest directed the work of other priests and Levites in the tabernacle or Temple. He himself performed certain important ceremonies, such as going into the most holy place once a year to make a sacrifice for the sin of the people. The high priest wore special clothing, described in Exodus 28; 39. Aaron was the first man to hold this office.

highminded. Too proud; conceited (1 Timothy 6:17).

Hilkiah (hil kī′ə). High priest during the reign of King Josiah. He found the lost book of the law in the Temple (2 Kings 22).

hin. Liquid measure; about one gallon (Exodus 29:40).

hind. Adult female deer.

hinder. Back; rear.

hindermost, hindmost. Farthest back.

Hiram (hī′rəm). Phoenician king of Tyre who sent his seamen with logs of cedar and cypress for King Solomon's building projects in Jerusalem.

hireling. Person hired for a job (John 10:12–13).

History. Two sections of Bible books. In the Old Testament these books are called History: Joshua, Judges, Ruth, 1 and 2 Samuel, 1 and 2 Kings, 1 and 2 Chronicles, Ezra, Nehemiah, Esther. (The Hebrews did not call these books history, nor are they the only Old Testament books with history in them.) In the New Testament the book of Acts is called History.

hither. Here.

hitherto. Till now.

Hittites (hit′īts). Powerful tribe that lived mainly in central Asia Minor (now central Turkey). Some Hittites lived among the Israelites; for instance, Uriah the Hittite was in King David's army.

Hivites (hiv′īts *or* hī′vīts). Probably same as the **Hurrians.**

hoar, hoary. Gray.

hoise. To hoist.

hold. Besides the more familiar meanings, also means a strongly fortified place, such as a fort (1 Samuel 22: 4) or a prison (Acts 4:3).

holiest. Same as **most holy place** (Hebrews 9:3).

holy. Belonging to God in a special sense; set apart for religious use; sacred.

Holy Ghost. Same as **Holy Spirit.**

Holy Land. Where Jesus lived on earth; **Palestine,** or parts of Israel and Jordan.

holy of holies. Same as **most holy place.**

Holy One. God.

holy place. Temple or tabernacle, especially the main inside room of it.

Holy Scriptures. Bible.

Holy Spirit (hō′li spir′it). God's Spirit; the unseen power of God that works through people's thoughts and feelings; the third person of the Trinity; same as **Holy Ghost, Comforter, Counselor,** and **Paraclete.**

Holy Writ. Bible.

homer. Dry measure, estimated between 3.8 and 6.6. bushels.

honor, honour. 1. Great respect given because of worth, wealth, fame, importance, and so on (1 Kings 3: 13). **2.** To have or show great respect for (Exodus 20:12).

Horeb (hō′reb). Same as **Sinai.**

horn. In early times horns of animals were used as blowing instruments and for holding oil. Often the word is used as a figure of speech for power (Luke 1:69).

hosanna. Save us, we pray thee! (Matthew 21:9).

Hosea (hō zā′ə). **1.** Prophet in Israel, the Northern Kingdom, about 750–

730 B.C. He seems to have had an unhappy home because of his wife's unfaithfulness, but details about this are not altogether clear. **2.** Old Testament book of the Minor Prophets, containing the prophecies of Hosea and some information about his life. Like Amos, Hosea preached about God's coming punishment upon sinful people. Unlike Amos, he also emphasized the love of God, who still wanted to help people if they would turn away from sin and obey him.

host. 1. Great number (Genesis 2:1). **2.** Army (Judges 4:2).

host of heaven. Stars and planets (Deuteronomy 4:19).

house. Often means family or household (Acts 16:31), or even descendants (Jeremiah 21:12).

householder. Head or master of a household.

howbeit. However.

Huldah (hul′də). Prophetess in Jerusalem who helped King Josiah (2 Kings 22:14).

Hurrians (hoor′i ənz). Tribe that lived in many places throughout the ancient Middle East; probably same as **Hivites.** The Hurrians once had a great kingdom near Haran, where Abraham once lived (now in southeastern Turkey).

husbandman. Farmer.

husbandry. Agriculture; farm work (1 Corinthians 3:9).

hypocrisy. In the Bible, means direct opposition to God (Matthew 23:28). It has since come to mean insincerity.

hypocrite. In the Bible, means a person who directly opposes God and God's work (Matthew 24:51). It has since come to mean an insincere person.

hyssop. Mintlike herb, used in religious ceremonies and in relieving pain.

Iconium (ī kō′ni əm). City in Galatia where Paul preached. Probably its church was one of those to which Paul wrote Galatians and Peter wrote 1 Peter. Today it is Konya, a provincial capital in central Turkey.

idol. Statue or other image of a god, that is worshiped. In the New Testament, people are sometimes called idol worshipers (idolaters) because they make something else in their lives (such as money) more important than God (Colossians 3:5).

ill. Wrong; wrongly (Genesis 43:6).

ill favoured. Poor in appearance (Genesis 41:3).

image. 1. Word used to describe the way man resembles God; usually thought to mean that man, like God, is a person; he can think, know, feel, and decide (Genesis 1:26). Jesus is mentioned as especially showing God's image (2 Corinthians 4:4). **2.** Picture of some-

hyssop

one (Mark 12:16). **3. Idol** (Daniel 3:1); same as **teraphim** (Genesis 31:19).

imagine. Often means to think and plan wrong deeds (Genesis 6:5; Psalm 2:1).

Immanuel (i man'yoo əl). "God is with us"—a name to be given to a special baby whose birth Isaiah predicted (Isaiah 7:14); same as **Emmanuel.** Matthew saw in the name a promise of God's coming to earth in the life of Jesus (Matthew 1:23).

immortal. Never dying; living forever.

immutable. Never changing; always the same.

impart. To give or share.

implead. To sue; to bring into court (Acts 19:38).

importunity. Begging or pleading; pestering.

impotent. Helpless because of handicap or illness; badly crippled (Acts 14:8).

impute. To consider something, good or bad, to be true of a person (Psalm 32:2).

inasmuch as. Because; since (Matthew 25:40).

incarnation. Taking on human form; especially means God's taking on human form as Jesus Christ.

incense. Mixture of spices and gums which is burned for the sweet smell it makes; used in the Hebrews' worship.

incline. To turn in the direction of; to have a tendency toward (Proverbs 2:2).

incorruptible. That which will not rot or decay.

increase. 1. To grow; to become greater (Luke 2:52). **2.** Addition; growth; especially, harvest of crops, birth of new domestic animals, and so on (Proverbs 3:9).

infidel. Person who does not believe or who has no religion.

infirmity. Weakness, sickness, or handicap.

Ingathering, Feast of. Same as "Booths, Feast of."

inhabit. To live in.

inherit. Besides the usual definitions, sometimes means to receive as a gift from God (Mark 10:17). The Israelites are also sometimes called God's inheritance (Isaiah 19:25). In the New Testament, Christians are called God's inheritance (Ephesians 1:18).

iniquity. Sin; wrong; often literally means something twisted out of its proper shape.

inn. In the Old Testament, this does not mean a hotel, but rather, just a place to spend the night; a camp; an oasis (Genesis 42:27). There were hotels in Judea of New Testament times (Luke 10:34), but they were very simple and crude.

innocence, innocency (in'ə s'n si). Freedom from guilt or wrong; especially, freedom from breaking God's laws (Psalm 73:13).

inquire of God, inquire of the Lord. To try to find God's will by praying, or by asking a priest or prophet (1 Samuel 9:9).

insomuch. So much.

inspiration. God's guidance of the people who wrote the Bible (2 Timothy 3:16).

inspire. To cause, urge, or influence to do something.

instantly. Earnestly (Luke 7:4).

insurrection. Rebellion; revolt.

integrity. Quality of being honest, sincere, upright; not two-faced or uncertain in one's thinking (Proverbs 11:3).

intercession. Asking in behalf of someone else (Jeremiah 36:25); especially, asking God (Hebrews 7:25).

interpretation. 1. Explanation of the meaning of something, such as a dream (Daniel 2:4). **2.** Translation into another language (John 1:42). **3.** Explanation of Bible truths (2 Peter 1:20).

intreat. Same as **entreat.**

iota. Smallest letter of the Greek alphabet, like the English letter *i;* same as **jot.**

Isaac (ī'zik). Son of Abraham and Sarah (Genesis 17:19). He was born according to God's promise when his parents were old. He obediently went with his father when Abraham thought God wanted him to sacrifice his son. Later, Isaac married his cousin Rebekah and had twin sons, Esau and Jacob.

Isaiah (ī zā'ə). **1.** Great prophet of Judah who lived about 760–690 B.C.; same as **Esaias.** During troubled times he urged people to trust in God, rather than in help from any foreign nation. God would take care of those who trusted him, and would some day send the Messiah—his great Saviour-King. Isaiah also spoke out boldly against wrong. Some people think he was finally killed by wicked King Manasseh. **2.** First book in the Major Prophets section of the Old Testament. It tells about Isaiah's life and includes many prophecies—Isaiah's own, and perhaps (as many people think) some of other inspired prophets as well. Chapters 1–39 tell about times before the fall of Jerusalem and the exile in Babylonia. Chapters 40–66 tell about times during and after the exile. Much of the book is written in magnificent poetry. It includes many great prophecies which—so Christians believe—came true in Jesus. Among these are Isaiah 9: 2-7; 11:1-9; 52:13 to 53:12.

Iscariot (is kar'i ət). Same as **Judas,** definition **1.**

Ish-bosheth (ish bō'shith). Son of King Saul who reigned over part of his dead father's kingdom; same as **Eshbaal.** He was a weak ruler. After a few years he was murdered, and his kingdom was joined to the rest of the country, over which David was already king (2 Samuel 2:8).

Ishmael (ish'mi əl). Son of Abraham and Hagar, his wife's Egyptian maid (Genesis 16:11). He was sent away, along with his mother, lest he, rather than Isaac, become Abraham's heir.

Ishmaelites, Ishmeelites (ish'mi ə-līts). Desert tribes that lived in what are now western Jordan, southern Syria, eastern Iraq, and northern Saudi Arabia. They were thought to be descended from Ishmael. Sometimes they seem to be the same people as the **Midianites** (Genesis 37:28; Judges 8:22-24).

Israel (iz'ri əl). **1.** Same as **Jacob,** definition **1** (Genesis 35:10). **2.** Hebrew nation—all descendants of **Jacob**-Israel; same as **Hebrews, Jews,** or **Israelites** (Deuteronomy 1:1). **3.** Kingdom ruled over by Saul, David, and Solomon (1 Kings 2:4). **4.** Northern Kingdom founded by Jeroboam I—actually a split from **Israel,** definition **3** (1 Kings 14:7). Its territory stretched from Dan (north of the Sea of Galilee) to Bethel (north of Jerusalem), and from the Mediterranean Sea to many miles east of the Jordan River. Some kings of Israel conquered other areas as well. However, the kingdom was never stable. Most of the rulers were wicked. Many came to the throne by murdering the former king and all his family. Assyria conquered the country in 721 B.C. **5.** Judah, the Southern Kingdom, after the Northern Kingdom had been destroyed (Isaiah 5:7). **6.** True people of God. In later Old Testament times, these people were Jews who trusted and obeyed God (Isaiah 49:6). In New Testament times and since, these people are Christians (Galatians 6:16). **7.** Modern republic, founded in 1948. It is called Occupied Palestine by Arab countries, which do not like to admit that it really exists. Its territory includes much of the strip of land between the Arabah and the Mediterranean Sea.

Israeli (iz rā'li). Having to do with **Israel,** definition **7;** a citizen of that country.

Israelite (iz'ri əl īt). Having to do with **Israel,** definition **2;** any **Hebrew** or **Jew.**

Issachar (is'ə kər). **1.** Ninth son of Jacob; ancestor of one of the twelve tribes of Israel (Genesis 30: 18). **2.** One of the smaller tribes of Israel (Joshua 17:10). Its territory was southwest of the Sea of Galilee.

issue. 1. To come or flow out (Joshua 8:22). **2.** Children; descendants (Matthew 22:25). **3.** Something which comes out, such as thoughts from the heart and mind (Proverbs 4:23).

issue of blood. Hemorrhage; continued bleeding.

Italy (it'ə li). Country in south central Europe, mainly on a long peninsula jutting into the Mediterranean Sea. In New Testament times it was part of the great Roman Empire, of which Rome was the capital. Aquila, Priscilla, and Paul were among the Christians who at one time or another lived in Italy (Acts 18:1–2; 27:1; 28:16,30).

it is written. Phrase meaning "It is written in the Old Testament" (Matthew 2:5).

Jabbok (jab'ək). Stream that flows through a deep canyon into the Jordan River about 15 miles north of the Dead Sea. At a ford of this stream, Jacob had an unusual nighttime experience with God (Genesis 32:22–32).

Jabesh (jā'bish), **Jabesh-gilead** (jā'-bish gil'i əd). City near the Jordan River, about 20 miles south of the Sea of Galilee. King Saul rescued Jabesh from the Ammonites. In return, the people of Jabesh gave a decent burial to the mistreated bodies of Saul and his sons. Only ruins (in Jordan) remain of Jabesh today, but the stream by which they lie is called Wādī al Yābis—"River of Jabesh."

Jacob (jā'kəb). **1.** Son of Isaac and younger twin brother of Esau (Genesis 25:27); also called **Israel.** He tricked Esau out of the birthright and the special blessing from their father. To escape Esau's revenge, he traveled to the northern Euphrates valley, married the sisters Leah and Rachel, started a large family, and grew rich. Later, he came back to Canaan and made up with his brother. His later life was sad because of the jealousy and wrong deeds of his sons. He died happy, however, because he was in the prosperous land of Egypt with all of his sons, who were friends with one another again. **2.** Descendants of Jacob; same as **Israel,** definition **2** (Psalm 14:7). **3.** God worshiped by Jacob; the true God (Psalm 24:6 in some translations).

Jacob's well

Jacob's Well. Well in Samaria (now in northwestern Jordan) where Jesus talked with a Samaritan woman (John 4:3–12). It is 75 feet deep; its water is cool and refreshing.

Jah (jä). Name for the Lord God; same as **Yahweh** (Psalm 68:4).

Jairus (jā ī′rəs). **Ruler of the synagogue** in a Galilean town, whose 12-year-old daughter was brought back to life by Jesus (Mark 5:22–43).

James (jāmz). Greek form of the Hebrew name Jacob; common name in New Testament times. There is much disagreement as to how many different Jameses the Bible mentions. Some people think that two or more of those listed in definitions **2–6** were the same man. **1.** Son of Zebedee and brother of John; one of Jesus' twelve apostles (Matthew 10:2). He and his brother and father fished together till Jesus called the two younger men. He became one of Jesus' closest friends. James was beheaded by King Herod Agrippa I in A.D. 44. **2.** Son of Alphaeus; one of Jesus' twelve apostles (Matthew 10:3). Almost nothing is known about him. **3.** Son of Mary and brother of Joses, known as James the Little—meaning that he was either small or young (Matthew 27:56; Mark 15:40). Many people think he was the same as **James,** definition **2.** **4.** Father or brother of Judas (not Iscariot), who was one of Jesus' twelve apostles (Luke 6:16). The Greek words literally read, "James's Judas." **5.** Half brother of Jesus (Galatians 1:19). He was not a follower of Jesus until after the resurrection. Later, he became one of the most important leaders among Christians of Jerusalem. **6.** Writer of the Bible book called James (James 1:1); many people think he was the same as **James,** definition **5.** **7.** New Testament book, placed second in the section called General Letters. It seems to have been written to Jews in general (James 1:1), but this verse probably means Christians in general. Its main point is this: a real Christian will do good and right deeds; a person who does not do such things is only pretending to be a Christian. James 1:22 is a key verse.

jangling. Noisy, useless discussion (1 Timothy 1:6).

javelin. Light spear (1 Samuel 19:10).

warrior with javelin

56

jealous. Sometimes means that God is concerned lest his people follow other gods (Psalm 78:58), or that a worshiper of God is concerned for the same reason (1 Kings 19: 10).

Jebusites (jeb'yə sīts). Tribe of Canaanites that lived in the strongly fortified city of Jerusalem. They held out against the Israelites until the time of King David. Some Jebusites continued to live there, among them, Araunah, who sold David the land on which the Temple was later built.

Jehoash (ji hō'ash). Same as **Joash.**

Jehoiada (ji hoi'ə də). High priest in Jerusalem who organized a rebellion against wicked Queen Athaliah and put the boy Joash, the true king, on the throne of Judah, the Southern Kingdom. He was Joash's uncle by marriage, and taught the boy to obey God's laws (2 Chronicles 23).

Jehoiakim (ji hoi'ə kim). King of Judah, the Southern Kingdom, about 609–598 B.C. (2 Kings 23:34–37). Unlike his father, Josiah, he was a bad king. He cut into shreds and burned the warning that the prophet Jeremiah sent him, and even tried to have Jeremiah killed. Probably Jehoiakim was murdered.

Jehoshaphat (ji häsh'ə fət *or* ji hō'-shə fət). King of Judah, the Southern Kingdom, about 873–849 B.C. He was a good and generally successful king who tried to follow God's will (2 Chronicles 17). A peacemaker, he brought to an end the 50-year war with Israel, the Northern Kingdom. He sent judges and teachers of the law to many cities.

Jehovah (ji hō'və). Name for the Lord God; same as **Yahweh** (Exodus 6:3).

Jehu (jē'hyōō). King of Israel, the Northern Kingdom, about 842–815 B.C. An army captain, Jehu received a message from the prophet Elisha that he should become king (2 Kings 9). He ruthlessly wiped out the royal family, including the king of Judah, the Southern Kingdom, who was a relative. He also killed many worshipers of Baal. Yet, Jehu himself was neither a loyal follower of the true God nor a successful ruler.

jeopardy. Danger.

Jephthah, Jephthae (jef'thə). One of the judges who rescued his fellow Hebrews from their enemies. He was a bandit chief when he was asked to fight the Ammonites. He made a foolish promise as a way of asking God's help in battle, and kept his promise by sacrificing his young daughter, an only child.

Jeremiah (jer'ə mī'ə), **Jeremias** (jer'ə mī'as), **Jeremy** (jer'ə mi). **1.** Great prophet of Judah, the Southern Kingdom, who lived about 650–580 B.C. He was born to a priestly family in Anathoth, near Jerusalem. Year after year he warned his fellow Jews that they would be punished for their sins, but few listened. Instead, they tried several times to silence or even kill the prophet. Jeremiah lived to see his sad predictions come true. After Jerusalem was captured, he was taken against his will to Egypt with some of the survivors, and died there. **2.** Old Testament book of the Major Prophets, giving many of Jeremiah's prophecies and much information about his life and times. Many of the prophecies are expressed in vivid, heartfelt poetry. A favorite and important passage is Jeremiah 31:31–34.

Jericho (jer'ə kō). Important city of the southern Jordan Valley, a few miles north of the Dead Sea. It is one of the oldest cities in the world; people lived there thousands of years before the time of Abraham. Old Testament Jericho was most famous for its walls that collapsed when Joshua and the Israelites attacked. New Testament Jericho, about a mile south of the old city, was the home of Zacchaeus and Bartimaeus, and the sunny winter capital of the country. Today the Jordanian town (called Arīḥā) has again been moved, a mile to the east.

Jeroboam (jer'ə bō'əm). **1.** Jeroboam I, founder of Israel, the Northern Kingdom. He led a revolt about 922 B.C. against Solomon's son, King Rehoboam. Jeroboam had to fight for the new kingdom throughout his reign. He set up new centers of worship at Bethel and at Dan, intending that his people should honor the true God there. Actually, however, both he and his people turned away from God. He was described as the man "that made Israel to sin" (1 Kings 11–16). **2.** Jeroboam II, who ruled Israel, the Northern Kingdom, about 786–746 B.C. (2 Kings 14:23). He was one of the most successful and prosperous of kings, but was not true to God. The prophets Amos and Hosea exposed the wrongs of his reign.

Jerubbaal (jer'ə bāl). Same as **Gideon.**

Jerusalem (jə rōō'sə ləm). Most important Hebrew city of Bible times; a national capital during various periods; the capital of Israel today (although the older parts of the city are in Jordan). Its location— on hills, near springs, at crossroads —has made it strategic from very early times. Abraham knew a king of **Salem** (Jerusalem). In Joshua's time the city was fortified by Jebusites who held out until conquered by King David. David then made Jerusalem his new capital, and did much to build the city. Solomon and Hezekiah were among the later kings who also enlarged or improved it. In 587 B.C. Jerusalem was captured and partly destroyed by Babylonian armies. Rebuilding began 50 years later, but the walls were not restored till 444. Herod the Great and other rulers had again made Jerusalem a fine city by the time Jesus was born. However, Caesarea was now the regular (Roman) capital, except during the Passover or other special occasions. As Jesus had predicted (Luke 19:41–44), Jerusalem was completely destroyed as a result of rebellion against the Romans. Again and again it has been rebuilt.

Jesse (jes'i). Father of David (1 Samuel 16:1); grandson of Boaz and Ruth.

Jesus (jē'zəs). Fairly common name in New Testament times; Greek form of the Hebrew name Joshua. **1.** Personal name of our Lord and Saviour, Jesus Christ, the Son of God. He was born to the virgin Mary in Bethlehem about 6 B.C. (Dates "before Christ" were not figured until many years later, and it seems that a mistake of several years was made.) Jesus' guardian or foster-father, Joseph, took him to Egypt to escape from jealous King Herod. Later, the family moved to Nazareth in Galilee, where Jesus lived until he was about 30. Only one event from his childhood or youth is known: the famous trip to the Temple in Jerusalem when he was 12. Joseph was a carpenter, and Jesus learned that trade. Probably he supported his mother and many younger half brothers and sisters after Joseph died. When he was about 30, Jesus left Nazareth, was baptized by John the Baptist, overcame temptations in the desert, moved to Capernaum, and began to preach and call disciples. For about three years he preached, taught, and healed—mainly in Galilee, but also in Judea, Samaria, and the territory east of the Jordan. Religious leaders of his time disagreed with many of his words and deeds, and opposed him more and more. At last, during Passover week (in April of about the year A.D. 30), he was betrayed in Jerusalem by one of his closest followers, given a mock trial, tortured, and executed like a common criminal. On the first day of the next week, he was raised from death by God's power. For about 40 days he appeared to his disciples and commanded them to tell all the world about him. Then he returned to his heavenly glory with God. **2.** Jewish friend of the apostle Paul (Colossians 4:11). **3.** Same as **Joshua** (Acts 7:45 and Hebrews 4:8 in some translations).

Jethro (jeth'rō). Priest of Midian; father-in-law of Moses (Exodus 3:1); same as **Reuel.**

Jew (jōō). **1.** Descendant of Abraham; same as **Hebrew** or **Israelite** (2 Kings 16:6). The word was not much used in this general meaning until after Israel, the Northern Kingdom, had been destroyed. **2.** Worshiper of the Lord God according to Jewish ideas and customs (Acts 14:1).

Jewry (jōō'rī). **1.** Same as **Judah,** definition **4** (Daniel 5:13), or **Judea** (Luke 23:5; John 7:1). **2.** Jewish people; Jews as a group (not a biblical term).

Jezebel (jez'ə bəl *or* jez'ə bel). Phoenician princess who married King Ahab of Israel, the Northern Kingdom. She was a wicked and strong-willed woman who tried to replace the worship of the Lord God with idol worship (1 Kings 16:31). She became the mother of two kings and one queen, but was killed horribly by followers of King Jehu.

Jezreel (jez'ri əl). **1.** Valley that runs from northwest to southeast, from the Mediterranean to the Jordan, and divides Galilee from Samaria (definition **2**). This is one of the most fertile areas in present-day Israel. **2.** Town in the valley of Jezreel. It was a favorite spot of King Ahab and his family; there he saw and took Naboth's vineyard. Today the Israeli town is called Yizre'el.

Joab (jō'ab). David's nephew (although they were probably close to the same age) and army commander (2 Samuel 2:18). He was brave and intelligent, and much of King David's success was due to his help. But Joab was also stubborn and cruel, and David at last turned against him. It was Joab who killed David's rebel son Absalom, against the king's orders. He also made the mistake of supporting the wrong prince as David's successor. King Solomon finally ordered his death.

Joash (jō'ash). Name (same as **Jehoash**) of several Bible characters, including two kings. The better known king ruled over Judah, the Southern Kingdom, about 837–800 B.C. He was saved in his cradle from his wicked grandmother, Queen Athaliah, who murdered all the other princes (2 Kings 11). When Joash was seven years old, the high priest Jehoiada led a revolt against Athaliah and put the little boy on the throne. As long as Jehoiada lived, Joash was a good king, but he seems to have changed later.

Job (jōb). **1.** Man of Old Testament

times who suffered many troubles but still kept his faith in God. He was rewarded for his loyalty. ("Patience," a word describing Job in some translations of James 5:11, really means steadfastness, or "stick-to-it-iveness.") **2.** Old Testament book that tells the story of Job. It is placed first in the section called Poetry, since only the first two and last one of its 42 chapters are in prose. The Hebrews called Job one of the Writings. Some of the world's finest poems—about birds, animals, weather, and countless other matters—may be found in Job's conversations with his friends and with God (chapters 3–41). No one knows exactly when or where Job lived, or who was inspired to write about him. The important thing is to try to learn God's message in the book. Two major thoughts seem to be these: (1) In spite of what some of Job's friends thought and said, suffering does not necessarily come as punishment for sin. (2) God's ways can never be fully understood.

Jochebed (jok′ə bed). Mother of Moses, Aaron, and Miriam (Numbers 26:59).

Joel (jō′əl). **1.** Prophet who probably lived in or near Jerusalem. Almost nothing else is known about him. **2.** Old Testament book of the Minor Prophets. In the first part of the book, Joel accurately describes a terrible plague of locusts. In the last part he goes on to describe God's day of judgment against wicked people, which will be far worse than any locust plague. At the same time Joel reminds people that God is loving and merciful, and will forgive and bless all those who trust in him.

John (jän). (See **John the Apostle, John the Baptist, John the Divine,** and **John the Elder.**) **1.** Relative of Annas the high priest (Acts 4:6). **2.** Same as **Mark** (Acts 12:12); his full name was John Mark. **3.** One of the Gospels, placed fourth in the New Testament. The book is unsigned, but many people believe that it was written by John the Apostle. (Some, however, think it was written by John the Elder.) John differs greatly from the other three Gospels. The others tell mainly about Jesus' work in Galilee; John tells much about his work in Judea and Samaria. The others tell more about what Jesus did and taught than about what he said to individuals; John includes long conversations with one or a few persons. John agrees with the others, however, in the really important matters—especially Jesus' death and resurrection. John's Gospel is careful to show that Jesus was truly the Son of God, with divine power, knowledge, and love. **4.** Three short New Testament books in the section called General Letters: 1 John, 2 John, and 3 John. Many people believe that they were written by John the Apostle (but some, that they were written by John the Elder). The first letter teaches that Christians should obey Christ, love one another, keep away from sin, and hold to true beliefs. The second letter warns against false teachers. The third letter encourages hospitality for missionaries. Third John is written to a man named Gaius; the other two are probably written to a church (called "the elect lady," a figure of speech, in 2 John).

John the Apostle (jän′ thē ə päs′'l). One of Jesus' twelve disciples (Mark 1:19). He was the son of Zebedee and Salome and the younger brother of James. The family probably lived in Capernaum and definitely fished for a living. Jesus called the two brothers to follow him, and they became his closest friends. Because of their hot tempers and stern ways, Jesus nicknamed them "sons of thunder." After the resurrection John was an active leader of the church in Jerusalem. If (as many people think) John is the **beloved disciple** (John 21:7), then we know much more about his life. He was an early follower of John the Baptist, had some special conversations with Jesus, and took care of Jesus' mother after the crucifixion. If (as many people think) John is the same man as the writer of Revelation (Revelation 1:9), then we know that he was exiled to the island of Patmos because he was a Christian. Ancient traditions say that he preached at Ephesus, lived to be very old, and was the only one of the twelve apostles to die a natural death.

John the Baptist (jän' thə bap'tist). Cousin, **Forerunner,** and baptizer of Jesus (Matthew 3:1; John 1:6). He was born as an answer to prayer, when his parents—Elizabeth and Zacharias the priest—were already old. When John grew up, he lived in the desert, probably so that he could think and pray without being disturbed. Then he began to urge people to turn away from their sins and to be baptized as a sign of this repentance. One day Jesus asked John to baptize him; John at first refused, but then did so. Later he was imprisoned and finally killed by Herod Antipas, because he attacked the sins of Antipas and his family.

John the Divine (jän' thə də vīn'). Writer of Revelation, called the Divine (or student of things about God) in the title of that book in some Bibles. In the book itself he simply calls himself John (Revelation 1:1). Many people believe he was the same as **John the Apostle.**

John the Elder (jän' thē el'dər). Early Christian leader who was said to have been taught by John the Apostle. He is not mentioned in the Bible, but some people think that he (not John the Apostle) was "the elder" who signed 2 John and 3 John.

Jonah (jō'nə), **Jonas** (jō'nəs). **1.** Prophet who lived during or before the time of Jeroboam II of Israel, the Northern Kingdom (2 Kings 14:25). His home was Gath-hepher, near Nazareth in Galilee. According to the book that bears his name, he went (unwillingly) at God's command to preach to the wicked city of Nineveh. **2.** Old Testament book of the Minor Prophets. It differs from all other books of prophecy in being almost entirely a story about a prophet instead of words spoken or written by a prophet. Many people believe that it was written to show that God loves all persons—that he is just as much concerned about foreigners (such as those in Nineveh) as about those who think they are God's special people (such as Jonah and his fellow Hebrews).

Jonathan (jän'ə thən). Name of many Old Testament characters, of whom the best known is David's great friend, the son of King Saul (1 Samuel 14:49). He loved David unselfishly, even though he knew that David, not he, might become the next king. He defended David against his jealous father, and even helped David to escape Saul's plots. He was a brave warrior and at last died fighting at his father's side.

Joppa (jäp'ə). Seaport 35 miles northwest of Jerusalem. Here King Solomon's workers landed the cedar logs that had been rafted down the coast for use in the Temple. In New Testament times the kind seamstress Dorcas was one of the first Christians there. Today Joppa is a part of the great Israeli city of Tel Aviv-Yafo.

that includes large areas east and south of the Jordan River and the Dead Sea, and smaller areas to the west of them. Its capital is 'Ammān.

Jordanian (jor dā′ni ən). Having to do with **Jordan,** definition **2;** a citizen of that country.

Joseph (jō′zəf). **1.** Next to the young-

Jordan River

Jordan (jôr′d'n). **1.** Longest and most important river in the area where most Bible events happened (Joshua 3:13). From its sources above the Sea of Galilee to its mouth at the Dead Sea is only 80 miles, but the Jordan crooks and turns for more than 200 miles. It begins as a swift, clear, mountain stream, but soon becomes muddy. It stays rather swift all the way and has many rapids. Its depth is from 3 to 10 feet; its width, about 100 feet—much wider in the springtime floods. There are at least 60 places where it can be waded across; these fords were of great importance in Bible times, since there were no bridges. Many stories center around this river; among them, the miraculous crossing by Joshua and the Israelites, and the baptism of Jesus. **2.** Modern Arab kingdom

est son of Jacob (Genesis 30:24). He was his father's favorite, and was sold into slavery in Egypt by his jealous older brothers. As an eventual result, he became prime minister of the country, saved part of several bumper crops, and so prepared for a famine that came later. When his brothers came to Egypt to buy grain, Joseph tested them to see whether they had changed. Then he brought them, his father, and all his relatives to live in Egypt. His two sons, Ephraim and Manasseh, were counted as ancestors of two tribes of Israel. **2.** Husband of Mary, mother of Jesus (Matthew 1:16). He was a carpenter and a good and kindhearted man. He became the father of Jesus' many half brothers and sisters. Probably he had died by the time Jesus was grown. **3.** Member of the Jewish Sanhedrin and native of the village of Arimathea, who buried Jesus in his own new tomb (Mark 15:43).

Joses (jō′ziz). One of Jesus' younger half brothers (Mark 6:3).

Joshua (jäsh′oo ə). **1.** Leader of the Israelites; same as **Oshea** and **Jesus,** definition 3. Joshua helped Moses and succeeded him. He was one of only two spies who thought the Israelites could conquer the land of Canaan (Numbers 13–14). After the 40 years of wandering, he was the general of the wars the Israelites fought in actually claiming that land. When he was old, he warned the Israelites one more time to remain true to God. **2.** Old Testament book of History, named after its main character. It tells how Joshua and the Israelites crossed the Jordan River, began to conquer Canaan, and then divided it up among the tribes. One of its most impressive stories is told in the last chapter: Joshua's challenge to his people to serve the Lord God. The key verse is Joshua 24:15. No one knows who wrote Joshua; many people think that more than one writer was inspired to do so.

Josiah (jō sī′ə). King of Judah, the Southern Kingdom, about 640–609 B.C. He was one of the best of all the kings. Only 8 years old when his wicked father died, he began while still young to try to do right and to lead his people back to God (2 Kings 22). During his reign a lost book of God's laws was found in the Temple. With this as the basis, Josiah started a national reform movement. Centers of false worship were destroyed. The Hebrews were urged to worship the true God. Josiah died in battle while still a young man.

jot. Same as **iota.**

joyful noise. Happy shout or song.

jubile, jubilee. Year of special celebration, when slaves were supposed to be set free; usually the fiftieth year.

Juda, Judah (jōō′də). **1.** Fourth son of Jacob and ancestor of one of the leading tribes of Israel (Genesis 29:35). He seems to have been less cruel than his brothers, for he spoke up once in behalf of Joseph and again in behalf of Benjamin. **2.** Tribe descended from Judah (Numbers 34:19). Its original territory was a small section south of Jerusalem (including Bethlehem), but other areas became attached to it. David and his royal descendants (including Jesus) came from the tribe of Judah. **3.** Southern Kingdom that was left to Rehoboam, Solomon's son, when ten of the tribes rebelled and set up Israel, the Northern Kingdom (2 Kings 3:1). It included a rather small area west and south of the Dead Sea. This smaller and less powerful kingdom, however, outlasted its northern neighbor. One reason why was that the kingship stayed in one family, instead of being tossed about among warring, murdering groups. The kingdoms separated about 922 B.C., and Judah lasted until it was conquered by Babylonia in 587 B.C. **4.** Province of the Persian Empire and later empires, after the Exile (Ezra 1:2); about the same area as **Judah,** definition 2.

Judaea (jōō dē′ə). Same as **Judea.**

Judaism (jōō′di iz′m). Religion of the Jewish people, based on a belief in the Lord God and the Old Testament (Galatians 1:13–14 in some translations).

Judaizer (jōō′di ī′zər). Jewish Christian who believed that Gentiles must become Jews in order to become Christians. Paul had many arguments with Judaizers.

Judas (jōō'dəs), **Jude** (jōōd). **1.** Judas **Iscariot,** one of Jesus' apostles, who betrayed his Lord (Matthew 10:4). He seems to have been the only one of the twelve from Judea, and was treasurer for the group. No one knows exactly why he turned against Jesus. Whatever the reason, he was sorry afterward, tried to return the payment for his treachery, and committed suicide. **2.** Another one of Jesus' apostles (Luke 6:16; John 14:22). He was the son or brother of some person named James. His other names may have been **Thaddaeus** and **Lebbaeus.** Little more is known about him. **3.** One of Jesus' younger half brothers (Mark 6:3). **4.** Writer of the letter of Jude (Jude 1); many people believe he was the same as **Jude,** definition **3. 5.** Jew in Damascus with whom Saul (Paul) stayed after his conversion on the road (Acts 9:11). **6.** Leading member of the church in Jerusalem (Acts 15:22–32). **7.** New Testament book, placed last in the section called General Letters. Its one chapter encourages Christians to keep their thinking straight about God and Christ, and warns fiercely against false teachers. Verse 3 sums up the little letter.

Judea (jōō dē'ə). Area mainly lying between the Dead Sea and Mediterranean Sea; sometimes included other areas as well; same as **Judaea.** The name was first used after the Exile, when it meant the same as **Judah,** definition **4.** Later, about 164 B.C., Judea became an independent kingdom. Its rulers conquered other nearby territories. Judea itself was conquered by the Roman Empire in 63 B.C. By Jesus' time it had shrunk again to the area between the two seas.

Thus it was one of the three main sections of the land west of the Jordan: Judea to the South, Galilee to the North, Samaria between.

Judges (juj'iz). Old Testament book of History. It tells about the Israelites from the death of Joshua till just before the birth of Samuel. It is named after several men (and one woman, Deborah) who "judged" the Israelites. This does not mainly mean that they decided legal cases, although some of them did so. It mainly means that they rescued their fellow Israelites from enemies who raided or captured them. The better known judges are Deborah and Barak, Gideon, Jephthah, and Samson. No one knows who wrote the book of Judges.

judgment. Often in Old Testament means justice—judgment that is right or fair (Psalm 33:5); "the judgment" (Luke 11:31–32) and "the day of judgment" (Matthew 10:15) mean God's judgment of people after death.

Julius (jōōl'yəs). Centurion who took Paul as a prisoner from Caesarea to Rome (Acts 27:1–3).

Jupiter (jōō'pə tər). Name used in some translations for **Zeus** (Acts 14:12).

justify. To make or declare a person to be right; usually means God's change in a person to make him right (Luke 18:14).

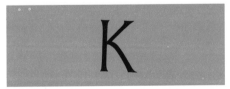

Kadesh (kā'dish), **Kadesh-barnea** (kā'dish bär'ni ə). Oasis where the Israelites camped on their way from Egypt to Canaan. From there the twelve spies were sent out. The spot today lies on the border of the United Arab Republic (Egypt), where three springs flow. One of them bears a form of the old name: 'Ain el Qadeis.

Kenites (kĕn′īts). Nomad tribe (similar to gypsies) that made its living by making, repairing, and sharpening metal objects. They may have also been called **Rechabites** or **Tishbites**. Kenites were usually friendly with Israelites.

key (kē). Usually a figure of speech for power or authority (Matthew 16:19).

Kidron (kid′rən). Valley (or brook) east of Jerusalem, dividing it from the Mount of Olives; same as **Cedron**. No water runs in it today except after heavy rains.

kindred. Relatives.

kine. Cows (Genesis 32:15).

kingdom of God, kingdom of heaven. Royal rule of God; not so much the area in which his rule works, as the fact itself that he is the supreme ruler.

Kings, 1 and 2. Two Old Testament books of History. They tell about the last days of King David; the reign of King Solomon; the divided kingdoms until the fall of Israel, the Northern Kingdom; the last years and fall of Judah, the Southern Kingdom; and a few later events. They also include the famous stories of Elijah, Elisha, and other prophets. The books stress the importance of worshiping the true God in right ways. Several other books are named as being sources used by the unknown but inspired writer (or writers) of 1 and 2 Kings.

kinsman. Relative.

Kiriath-jearim (kir′ə ath jē′ə rim), **Kirjath-jearim** (kūr′jath jē′ə rim). City 8 miles west of Jerusalem (now in Israel) that belonged to the clever Gibeonites, and so was not destroyed by the Israelites (Joshua 9). Once the ark of the covenant was kept there.

Kish (kish). Father of King Saul.

Kishon (kī′shən *or* kish′ən). River that flows northwestward through the valley of Jezreel north of Mount Carmel, and into the Mediterranean Sea. Although parts of it run dry in hot weather, it is hard to cross in springtime floods. Probably flooded, marshy ground helped Barak to defeat the Israelites' enemies near the Kishon (Judges 4:13–15; 5:19–21).

kiss. Usual way of welcoming (and of saying good-by to) someone of either sex—much as a handshake is today.

kneading bowl, kneading trough. Vessel of wood, bronze, or clay, in which dough was kneaded.

Kohath (kō′hath). Second son of Levi, whose descendants included Moses, Aaron, Miriam, and men who carried the tabernacle and ark of the covenant from place to place (Exodus 6:16).

Koheleth (kō hē′ləth). Name that the writer of Ecclesiastes used for himself (Ecclesiastes 1:1); sometimes translated "the **Preacher.**"

Korah (kôr′ə). **1.** Israelite who led a revolt against Moses and died as a result (Numbers 16). **2.** Forefather of an important group of musicians in the Temple (titles of Psalms 42; 44; 47; 48; 87).

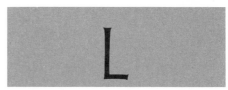

Laban (lā′bən). Brother of Rebekah, Isaac's wife; father of Rachel and

Leah, Jacob's wives. He gave Jacob a job tending his flocks and herds. Each man tried to outtrick the other. Finally they swore to leave each other alone (Genesis 31:42–55).

Lachish (lā′kish). City halfway between Jerusalem and Gaza (now in Israel); one of the more important cities of Judah in Old Testament times. It has not been lived in since about 150 B.C.

lamb. Since young sheep were often used as sacrifices, Jesus is sometimes spoken of as a lamb (1 Peter 1:18–19) or the Lamb of God (John 1:29), because he sacrificed his life for the whole world.

lament. To feel or show deep sorrow; to mourn with tears.

Lamentations (lam′ən tā′shənz). Old Testament book, placed third in the section called Major Prophets, although it is really a book of poems. Each of the five chapters is a separate poem. All of them mourn (or *lament*) the capture of Jerusalem in 587 B.C. Lamentations is placed after Jeremiah in the Bible, because for centuries many people have thought that Jeremiah wrote the poems. Actually, no one knows who was inspired to do so.

ancient oil lamp

lamp. Clay pitcher filled with olive oil, with a wick lying in the spout; called **candle** in some translations.

lampstand. Clay or metal base for a lamp or lamps; called **candlestick** in some translations.

Last Supper. Last meal Jesus ate with his disciples before he was crucified; the first **Lord's Supper.**

latchets on sandals

latchet. Leather thong or strap by which sandals are tied.

Latin (lat′'n). Official language of the Romans; it was one of the three languages in which the title on Jesus' cross was written (John 19:20).

latter rain. Showers in April and May that brought the usual rainy season to an end; same as **spring rain** (James 5:7).

laud. To praise highly.

laugh to scorn. To make fun of; to laugh in a mocking way (Matthew 9:24).

lavers

laver. Large bowl or vessel to wash in, especially those used for ceremonial washings in the tabernacle and the Temple (Exodus 30:18; 1 Kings 7:38).

law. 1. Any rule which must be obeyed, whether decided by man (Genesis 47:26) or by God (Genesis 26;5). **2.** All of God's rules (Psalm 1:2). **3.** God's rules in the Old Testament, plus other rules added by Jewish scribes (John 18: 31). **4.** First five books of the Old Testament; usually capitalized, except in some translations of the Bible (Luke 10:26). Law is a major division both in English Bibles and Hebrew Bibles (the other Hebrew divisions being **Prophets** and **Writings**). These books include many things besides laws, but they do contain many laws, especially in Exodus, Leviticus, Numbers, and Deuteronomy. **5.** Entire Old Testament (1 Corinthians 14:21); more often, the term used for this meaning is "the law and the **prophets"** (Matthew 22:40).

lawyer. Expert in Jewish law; scribe (Luke 10:25).

lay hands on. 1. To capture (Mark 14:46). **2.** To set aside an animal for sacrifice by putting one's hands on it (Leviticus 4:4). **3.** To touch someone in the act of blessing him —with words (Matthew 19:15), or with healing (Mark 6:5). **4.** To touch someone, thus ceremonially setting him aside to do special work for God (Acts 13:3).

Lazarus (laz′ə rəs). **1.** Brother of Mary and Martha who was raised from death by Jesus (John 11:5, 43). This family, whom Jesus especially loved, lived in Bethany, near Jerusalem. **2.** Sick beggar in one of Jesus' parables (Luke 16: 20).

league. Alliance; covenant.

Leah (lē′ə). Older daughter of Laban, sister of Rachel, and first wife of Jacob (Genesis 29:16). Laban tricked Jacob into marrying weak-eyed Leah first, when it was really beautiful Rachel that he loved. Leah became the mother of six sons and one daughter.

leathern. Made of leather.

leaven. 1. Lump of left-over dough, mixed with the next batch of dough to make it rise (Luke 13:21). There was no true yeast in Bible times. **2.** Anything that causes a change in something far larger than itself—either for good (Matthew 13:33), or for bad (1 Corinthians 5:6).

Lebanon (leb′ə nən). **1.** Range of mountains that follows the Mediterranean coast north of Galilee (Deuteronomy 1:7). It was most famous in Bible times for its magnificent cedar trees (Psalm 104:16), of which few remain today. The mountains are still called Jabal Lubnān. The name means white; the peaks, ranging from 6,000 to 11,000 feet, are often snowcapped. **2.** Modern republic; its small territory is bounded by the Mediterranean Sea on the west, Israel on the south, and Syria on the east and north.

Lebbaeus (le bē′əs). Another name for **Thaddaeus** (Matthew 10:3); possibly the same man as **Judas,** definition **2**; one of Jesus' apostles.

legion. Division in the Roman army; usually 6,000 men. The word came to mean any large number of persons (Mark 5:9).

lentiles

lentiles, lentils. Types of beans or peas used in making a reddish-

67

brown stew or **pottage** (Genesis 25: 34).

leper. Person who has **leprosy.**

leprosy. General name for several types of serious skin diseases, including leprosy as we know it today (Hansen's disease). People who were leprous in the worst sense had to stay away from others and shout, "Unclean!" when anyone came too near. They had open sores, white scabs, lack of feeling in parts of their bodies, and finally loss of those parts. However, not all persons called lepers in the Bible seem to have had quite so serious an illness. Naaman, for instance, was still able to live with his family (2 Kings 5).

lest. For fear that.

let. Besides the usual meanings, sometimes means prevented or hindered (Romans 1:13).

Levi (lē'vī). **1.** Third son of Jacob (Genesis 29:34). Among his descendants were Moses, Aaron, Miriam, and all the priests and Levites. **2.** Tribe descended from Levi (Numbers 18:2). They were not given an area as were the other tribes, and so are not usually listed as one of the twelve tribes. Instead, they were given special cities scattered throughout the other tribal areas. **3.** Probably the same as **Matthew** (Luke 5:27–32).

leviathan. Huge water animal of some unknown type (Job 41).

Levites (lē'vīts). Members of the tribe of Levi; especially, those who helped the priests in the tabernacle or the Temple. All priests were Levites, but not all Levites were priests. Levites carried the tabernacle from place to place, kept the holy vessels clean, sang in the Temple choir, and helped the priests in other ways.

Leviticus (lǝ vit'i kǝs). Old Testament book of Law. As the name suggests, it has much to say about the work of Levites and priests. Except for four brief descriptions of events that had something to do with laws, the entire book is a collection of laws and of instructions about sacrifices. Leviticus and Psalms have been compared like this: Leviticus is the order of service for Hebrew worship, while Psalms is the hymnal that was used. One of the most important of all Bible verses, according to Jesus, is Leviticus 19:18. (See Luke 10:25–27).

Libertines (lib'ǝr tēnz). Same as **Freedmen** (Acts 6:9).

lice. Probably gnats or mosquitoes, rather than the plural form of "louse" (Exodus 8:16–18).

license. Permission (Acts 21:40; 25: 16).

licentiousness. Immorality; especially, wrong sexual thoughts or deeds.

light. Besides the usual meanings, often means that which is right, good, pleasing to God (John 3:20), as compared to **darkness.**

likeminded. Having the same thoughts or attitudes as another person (Philippians 2:2,20).

liken. To compare.

likeness. Condition of looking or being like someone or something else.

liketh. Pleases (Esther 8:8).

likewise. In the same way.

lilies. General name that Jesus used for the brilliant red and yellow flowers that dot the hillsides of Galilee in early spring (Matthew 6:28). The anemone, the ranunculus, and the poppy may have been among the flowers he had in mind.

lineage. Ancestry; line of descent; tribe (Luke 2:4).

list. To wish or choose (John 3:8).

living water. Running water in a stream, as compared to water stored in a tank or cistern (Jeremiah 2: 13). Jesus used living water as a figure of speech for the new life he gives to those who trust in him (John 4:10–11).

lo. Look! See! (Luke 2:9.)

locust

locust. Large insect like a grasshopper. Often it wanders in huge swarms, destroying crops. In Bible times it was considered a delicious food (Mark 1:6). Some people in the Middle East still eat locusts today, mixing them with honey.

Lod (läd). Same as **Lydda.**

lodge. To spend the night.

loins. Hips and lower part of the back and abdomen. When a man had to run, fight, or do some other hard job, he would "gird up his loins"; that is, gather up the long skirts of his outer robe so that they would not get in his way.

Lois (lōʹis). Timothy's grandmother (2 Timothy 1:5).

longsuffering. 1. Patient; slow to become angry (Psalm 86:15). **2.** Patience (Romans 2:4).

looking glass. Mirror, actually made of metal in Bible times (Job 37: 18; Exodus 38:8).

lord. 1. Master; ruler (1 Kings 11:23). **2.** General title of respect or honor, like our "sir" (Matthew 8:6). **3.** Special name for God (usually capitalized), showing that he is ruler of all things and all people (Psalm 77:11); see also **Yahweh. 4.** Special name for Jesus (Romans

10:9); when someone called Jesus "Lord" (in this sense), it was the same as admitting that he was God as well as man.

Lord of hosts. Special title for God, meaning Ruler of Armies. Same as Lord of **Sabaoth.**

Lord's Day. Sunday.

Lord's Prayer. Prayer that Jesus gave as a model, recorded in Matthew 6:9–13. A shorter and slightly different version is given in Luke 11: 2–4.

Lord's Supper. 1. Memorial Supper established during the meal that Jesus had with his apostles before the crucifixion; same as **Last Supper.** He commanded that his followers continue to eat bread and drink from the cup to remind themselves of his body and blood that were sacrificed for them. **2.** Any observance of the special meal that Jesus asked his followers to continue as a memorial to him.

Lot (lät). Nephew of Abraham who traveled with his uncle from the Tigris-Euphrates Valley to Canaan (Genesis 11:31). When his shepherds and Abraham's shepherds quarreled because there was too little grass and water for both flocks, Abraham gave Lot first choice of a location. Lot settled near Sodom, and later had several

ancient looking glasses

family tragedies because of the wicked people who lived there.

lots. Two or more objects, of which one is drawn out or thrown out without looking, to decide some question; similar to drawing straws. Lots were used in gambling (Matthew 27:35). However, many people believed that God decided which lot would come out first (Proverbs 16:33). Thus they sometimes used this method of finding God's will, both in Old Testament times (Jonah 1:7) and in New Testament times (Acts 1:26). See also **Thummim.**

lovingkindness. Loyal or **steadfast love;** the kind of love that only God can be depended upon to show.

low country, low plains. Same as **Shephelah.**

Lucas (lo͞o′kəs). Same as **Luke,** definition **1** (Philemon, verse 24).

Lucifer (lo͞o′sə fər). Word in Isaiah 14:12 that is translated Day Star in some versions. The name is now sometimes used for the **devil.**

lucre. Riches; money.

Luke (lo͞ok). **1.** Doctor who was Paul's close friend and helper on missionary trips. He is mentioned only three times in the Bible: Colossians 4:14, 2 Timothy 4:11, and Philemon 24. Probably he was a Gentile rather than a Jew—the only Gentile to write part of the Bible. His two books, Luke and Acts, make up a longer part of the New Testament than that written by any other one person. Sections of Acts that use such words as "we" and "us" tell about some of Luke's missionary work with Paul. Paul seems to have had much sickness; perhaps only Luke's loving care kept him alive. **2.** New Testament book of biography; third of the four Gospels. Some people think that Luke collected materials for

his book about Jesus while Paul was in prison for two years at Caesarea. Luke was inspired to include many stories not told in any other Gospel. Some people think he learned about these events by interviewing persons who took part in them— perhaps including Jesus' mother, since he tells more about Jesus' birth and childhood than any other writer. Luke's Gospel shows Jesus as the Saviour for everyone.

lunatick. Epileptic (Matthew 4:24 in some translations).

LXX. Abbreviation for **Septuagint.**

Lycaonia (lik′i ō′ni ə *or* lī′ki ō′ni ə). Part of Galatia (now in south central Turkey). Its main cities were Lystra and Derbe (Acts 14:6). The Lycaonian language was still being spoken when Paul and Barnabas came there as missionaries (Acts 14:11).

Lydda (lid′ə). Town northwest of Jerusalem where Peter healed a paralyzed man and won many people to Christ (Acts 9:32). Today the town is known by the Old Testament form of its name: **Lod.** Nearby is one of Israel's most important airports.

Lydia (lid′i ə). Businesswoman of Philippi who may have been the first Christian in Europe. She imported and sold fine purple-dyed cloth from her former home, Thyatira in Lydia. Her home became Paul's headquarters in Philippi and the first meeting place of the church he founded there (Acts 16:14–40).

lyre. Type of small **harp.**

Lysias, Claudius (klô′di əs lis′i əs). Roman tribune in Jerusalem who rescued Paul from a mob and sent him to Caesarea to be tried (Acts 23:26).

Lystra (lis′trə). City of Galatia (now in south central Turkey). Paul visited there on his first and second missionary journeys. He took from there a new helper: young Timothy, whose mother and grandmother must have been among Lystra's first believers in Christ. Only a mound of ruins remains of Lystra today.

Macedonia (mas'ə dō'ni ə). Country north of Achaia (Greece); Roman province in New Testament times. Philippi, Thessalonica, and Beroea were among its cities in which Paul preached. He first came there because he saw in a dream a Macedonian who invited him. Today Macedonia is part of Greece, of Bulgaria, of Yugoslavia, and of Albania.

Machaerus (mə kir'əs). Fortress east of the Dead Sea where John the Baptist may have been imprisoned and beheaded; not named in the Bible. Machaerus was the second strongest Jewish castle, next to Antonia in Jerusalem. Now in Jordan, its ruins are called Mukāwir.

Mach-pelah (mak pē'lä). Cave that Abraham bought from the Hittites to use as a family cemetery. It was close to **Mamre** and **Hebron,** in the hills southwest of Jerusalem (now in Jordan).

Madian (mā'di ən). Same as **Midian.**

Magdala (mag'də lə). Fishing town at the westernmost point of the Sea of Galilee; home of Mary Magdalene. The nearby Israeli community is still called Migdal.

Magi (mā'jī). Same as **Wise Men.**

magistrate. Judge; ruler.

Magnificat (mag nif'ə kat). Mary's song in Luke 1:46–55, so called because of its first word in the Latin Bible.

magnify. To make great or announce as being great (Psalm 34:3).

Magog (mā'gäg). See **Gog and Magog.**

Mahanaim (mā'ə nā'əm). City east of the Jordan River, twice used as headquarters for a king who had to escape from the main part of the country. Ish-bosheth, Saul's son, reigned there briefly. David stayed there while his rebellious son Absalom held Jerusalem. No one knows exactly where in Jordan the city was.

Mahlon (mä'lən). Naomi's son and Ruth's first husband (Ruth 1:2).

maid, maiden. 1. Young unmarried girl or woman (Exodus 2:8). **2.** Female servant (Exodus 2:5).

maidservant. Female slave.

mail. Armor worn by a soldier (1 Samuel 17:5).

majesty. Dignity; power.

Malachi (mal'ə kī). **1.** Old Testament prophet who lived, preached, and wrote about 450 B.C. He lived in or near Jerusalem. His name means messenger, and some people think it was a title rather than a real name. Nothing more is known about him. **2.** Last book of the Old Testament and of the Minor Prophets section. Its four short chapters are mainly written in question and answer form. The book shows the importance of being honest and sincere in worship, and of giving God one's best in tithes and offerings. It also predicts that someone will come to announce the Messiah, followed by the Messiah himself.

Malchus (mal'kəs). Servant of the high priest; his ear was cut off by Peter when he came to arrest Jesus. Jesus healed him (John 18: 10).

malefactor. Criminal.

malice, maliciousness (mə lish'əs nis). Spite; hate; feeling of wanting to hurt someone.

Malta (môl'tə). Island in the Mediterranean Sea, south of Sicily; same as **Melita.** Here Paul was shipwrecked on his way to Rome, and spent three months teaching and healing.

mammon. Wealth; property.

Mamre (mam'ri). Place southwest of Jerusalem where Abraham and his descendants often camped; about 1-2/3 miles north of **Hebron,** and just west of **Mach-pelah,** the family cemetery. Great trees grew there—either oaks or pistachio-nuts. The site is now in Jordan.

Manaen (man'i ən). Relative or close friend of Herod Antipas who became a Christian leader at Antioch in Syria (Acts 13:1).

Manasseh (mə nas'ə). **1.** Older son of Joseph and an Egyptian mother. He was "adopted" by his grandfather Jacob and so counted as the forefather of one of the twelve tribes of Israel (Genesis 41:51). **2.** Tribe of Israel, actually divided into two great half-tribes (Joshua 12:6). Both settled north of the Jabbok River—one east, the other west of the Jordan River. **3.** King of Judah, the Southern Kingdom, beginning about 687 B.C. (2 Kings 21:1). Although his father was good King Hezekiah, Manasseh was one of the most wicked of kings. He came to the throne when he was only twelve, and had a long, cruel reign. Once he was captured and taken to Babylon, but was allowed to return home.

mandrakes. Wild plants whose plum-like berries and fleshy roots were eaten by women, supposedly to help them have children.

manger. Trough or box out of which farm animals eat.

manifest. Well known; shown; revealed.

manifold. Having many forms or of many kinds.

manna. Food which God provided for the Israelites in the desert. It was sweet and whitish.

manner. 1. Way; custom (Hebrews 10:25). **2.** Kind; sort (2 Kings 1:7).

Manoah (mə nō'ə). Samson's father.

manservant. Male slave.

mansion. Place to stay; room (John 14:2).

mantle. Word used for various pieces of clothing; usually an outer robe, coat, or cloak.

manuscript. Anything written by hand; especially, handwritten copies of Bible books.

Maon (mā'ən). Hometown of Nabal and Abigail, south of Jerusalem; their flocks were pastured in nearby Carmel (now in Jordan).

Mara (mar'ə). Name that means bitter.

Maranatha (mar'ə nath'ə). Probably a motto or password among early Christians; an Aramaic phrase meaning, "Come back soon, our Lord!" (See 1 Corinthians 16:22.)

Marcus (mär'kəs). Same as **Mark.**

mariner. Sailor.

Mark (märk). **1.** Early follower of

mandrake plant and root

Jesus (Acts 12:12); same as **Marcus** and **John,** definition **1.** He left his home in Jerusalem to go with Paul and Barnabas—first to Antioch in Syria, then on their first missionary journey, which he quit before it was over. Paul refused to take him on another trip, but Barnabas, Mark's relative, worked with Mark on Cyprus. Later Paul agreed that Mark had become a dependable worker. He also worked with Peter, perhaps in Rome. From early times many people have believed that Peter was Mark's main human source in writing his book about Jesus. **2.** Second book of the New Testament. Many people believe, however, that it was the first of the four Gospels to be written. It is the shortest of the four; yet, in the stories it tells, Mark includes many details left out by the others. It is a fast-moving book, concerned mainly with Jesus' deeds. It tells nothing about his early years, but much about his ministry, especially the last days leading up to his death.

mark. To notice or pay attention to (1 Kings 20:7).

market, marketplace. 1. Everywhere except in the book of Acts, means a street of shops, like bazaars in oriental towns of today (Luke 7: 32). **2.** In the book of Acts, means the public square in a Greek city, surrounded by temples, courthouses, and other such buildings (Acts 16:19).

Mars' Hill (märz' hil'). Same as **Areopagus.**

Martha (mär'thə). One of Jesus' friends who lived at Bethany (just east of Jerusalem); sister of Mary and Lazarus. Martha was the practical, hard-working member of the family. Jesus even had to warn her once that other things were more important than getting everyday jobs done (Luke 10:38).

martyr. Person who witnesses to his faith in Jesus by being willing even to die for it.

marvel. To wonder; to be surprised.

Mary (mer'i *or* mar'i). Common name in New Testament times; same name as Miriam in the Old Testament. Some people think that the women described here in definitions **2** and **3** were the same; also, the women in definitions **4** and **5.** Neither of these ideas can be proved. **1.** Jesus' mother, the **virgin** Mary (Luke 1:27). Mary's hometown was Nazareth in Galilee. Nothing is known of her early years. She was betrothed (more than engaged but less than married) to Joseph, a carpenter. God sent the angel Gabriel to tell her that by a miracle she would become the mother of God's Son. The baby was born while Mary and Joseph were in Bethlehem, registering for a Roman census. Mary noticed the many unusual happenings after Jesus' birth, and thought about them privately. The young family moved to Egypt, then back to Nazareth. There Mary became the mother of four more boys and at least two girls. Probably she became a widow before Jesus began his public work. Like Jesus' brothers, Mary did not fully understand or accept what Jesus was trying to do. Yet, she was loyal enough to stand by the cross when he was dying. After the resurrection she became one of his followers. Nothing more is known of her life. **2.** Mary Magdalene (meaning "from Magdala"), one of Jesus' followers (Mark 16:1), out of whom he had driven seven devils. She was one of the first people to see Jesus after the resurrection. **3.** One of

Jesus' friends who lived at Bethany (just east of Jerusalem); sister of Martha and Lazarus (John 11:1). She was a quiet, thoughtful person who saw more fully than many others the importance of Jesus, and showed how she felt by listening to him and by anointing him. **4.** Mother of James the Little, one of Jesus' apostles (Mark 16:1); faithful follower of Jesus who saw him crucified and buried, but also raised again. **5.** Wife or daughter of Clopas (actually, "Clopas' Mary"), who stood near Jesus' cross with his mother (John 19:25). **6.** Mother of John Mark (Acts 12:12); early Christian of Jerusalem who let her fellow believers meet in her large house.

Master. When used by someone speaking to Jesus, usually means teacher or rabbi.

Matthew (math'yoo). **1.** One of Jesus' twelve apostles (Matthew 9:9; 10:3); probably his other name was **Levi**. He was a tax collector when Jesus called him to follow. He then gave a great feast for Jesus and invited other tax collectors. Almost nothing more is known about him, except the belief from early times that he wrote one of the Gospels. **2.** First book of the New Testament, and of the section called Biography. For many centuries most Christians thought Matthew was the first Gospel to be written. More people now think that Mark was first. Matthew was inspired to include many of Jesus' teachings not written anywhere else, and to arrange them in careful groupings. He also gave special attention to showing that Jesus was the Christ, the Messiah, in whom the Old Testament prophecies came true. He quoted more Old Testament verses than any other

New Testament writer. Only Matthew tells about the Wise Men, lists all of Jesus' Beatitudes, and gives a full account of the Sermon on the Mount.

Matthias (mə thī'əs). Early Christian who was chosen to take the place of Judas Iscariot among the twelve apostles (Acts 1:26).

Mazzaroth (maz'ə räth). Probably means the constellations of stars called the twelve signs of the zodiac.

meal. Rough, coarse flour—made either of barley or of whole wheat; not corn meal (1 Kings 17:12). Ordinary people in Bible times used far more meal than fine flour.

meal offering. Same as **meat offering.**

meat. Often means food of any kind (Genesis 1:29).

meat offering. Sacrifice of bread or the ingredients for it; same as **meal offering.** Sometimes it was entirely burned on the altar; sometimes part of it was saved for the priests to eat. See also **sacrifice.**

Medes (mēdz). Tribe that lived in an area which is now northwestern Iran and nearby parts of the Soviet Union. They were conquered by Cyrus, king of Persia. His kingdom was then sometimes called that of the Medes and the Persians.

mediator. Someone who acts as a go-between and tries to bring two persons or groups together. Jesus is the "one mediator between God and men" (1 Timothy 2:5).

meditate. To think or plan; to think quietly.

meek, the. People who depend on God instead of on themselves—who they are or what they have.

meet. Right; fitting; proper (Luke 15:32; 1 Corinthians 15:9).

Megiddo (mə gid'ō). Important city that overlooks the valley of Jezreel. It has been a battlefield many times. Barak won a victory there; many years later, King Josiah lost his life there. The modern Israeli town, a little to the south, still has the old name.

Melchisedec, Melchizedek (mel kiz'ə-dek'). King and priest of Jerusalem in ancient times (Genesis 14:18). Little is known about him. Since the Christ is also described as both king and priest, the writers of Psalm 110 and of the book of Hebrews compare Christ and Melchizedek.

Melita (mə lē'tə). Same as **Malta.**

Melzar (mel'zär). Title (not really the name) of a steward or overseer in the royal Babylonian court.

members. 1. Parts of a body (James 3:5-6). 2. Fellow Christians (1 Corinthians 12:26).

menorah. Seven-branched lampstand (called a candlestick in some translations) that was used in the tabernacle and in the Temple. It has become one of the religious symbols of modern Judaism.

Mephibosheth (mi fib'ə shith). Crippled son of Jonathan (2 Samuel 4:4). King David gave Mephibosheth a place of honor in his court.

Merab (mir'ab). King Saul's oldest daughter, who was promised to David, but married to another man (1 Samuel 14:49).

Mercurius (mər kyoor'i əs). Name (same as Mercury) used in some translations for **Hermes** (Acts 14:12).

mercy. Feelings of love, sympathy, forgiveness, help, or any combination of these.

mercy seat. Special cover for the ark of the covenant. It was made of gold and had two statues of cherubim. Its name meant that this was the place where the God of mercy would especially take his seat and forgive those who asked.

Meshach (mē'shak). One of three young Hebrew captives in Babylon who were thrown into a blazing furnace because they would worship no one but the true God (Daniel 3).

Mesopotamia (mes'ə pə tā'mi ə). "Between the Rivers"—the whole area of the Tigris-Euphrates Valley.

mess (mes). Serving of food (Genesis 43:34).

Messiah (mə sī'ə), **Messias** (mə sī əs). Hebrew word meaning the same as the Greek word **Christ** (John 4:25).

mete. To measure.

Methuselah (mə thoō zə lə). Noah's grandfather; said to have lived 969 years, the longest life mentioned in the Bible (Genesis 5:27).

mezuzah on doorpost

mezuzah. Hebrew word for doorpost or door, which later came to mean the small box attached to a doorpost, containing copies of Old Testament verses; see **phylacteries.**

Micah (mī'kə). 1. Prophet of Judah, the Southern Kingdom, who lived about 750–700 B.C. in Moresheth-gath, a village southwest of Jerusalem (Jeremiah 26:18). He was interested in country folk and their hard times, and announced that God would punish the wicked people of Jerusalem. 2. Old Testament book of the Minor Prophets, containing the prophecies of Micah. Important verses are 6:8 (which tells what God expects of those who worship him) and 5:2 (which predicts that the Christ would be born in Bethlehem).

Micaiah (mi kā′yə *or* mī kā′yə). Prophet of Israel, the Northern Kingdom, who warned King Ahab of defeat and death in battle about 850 B.C. He was brave enough to speak the truth, even though false prophets were telling lies that they knew the king wanted to hear. (2 Chronicles 18:12–16.)

Michael (mī′k′l). Familiar Hebrew name, given to one of the archangels (Daniel 12:1).

Michal (mī′k′l). King Saul's younger daughter who became David's first

defeated the Midianites so soundly that they never bothered his people again.

mighty acts, mighty deeds. Miracles.

mighty men. Strong, brave, proud heroes.

mighty works. Miracles.

Milcom (mil′kəm). Same as **Molech.**

mile. Roman mile, 142 yards shorter than our mile (Matthew 5:41).

Miletus (mī lē′təs). Great seaport of Roman times, south of Ephesus in the province of Asia (now western Turkey). There Paul met the leaders of the church at Ephesus, as he was on his way to Jerusalem. Miletus' harbor, like Ephesus', filled with silt, and ruins of the city now lie 5 miles from the sea.

mill. Two stones between which grain

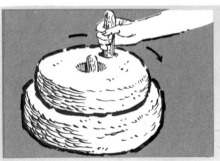 

types of mills

wife (1 Samuel 14:49). She helped David escape from her jealous father, but then was given to another husband. When David became king, he reclaimed Michal.

Midian (mid′i ən), **Midianites** (mid′-i ən ītz′). Desert tribe (same as **Madian**) that lived in what is now northwestern Saudi Arabia, but often made raids into other areas. Sometimes they seem to be the same tribe as the **Ishmaelites** (Genesis 37:28; Judges 8:22–24). Moses lived with the Midianites for many years, and married a Midianite wife. Later, the Israelites and Midianites were enemies. Gideon at last

was ground into meal or flour. In Old Testament times, the lower (or nether) **millstone** was a rectangular block about 30 inches long; the upper millstone, much smaller, was rubbed back and forth on it (Exodus 11:5; Isaiah 47:2). In New Testament times, both millstones were round, and the upper one often had a hole in the middle (Matthew 18:6; 24:41). The top stone was turned to do the grinding. Throughout Bible times, grinding was a job a woman in each family had to do every morning. Animals were used to turn stones of large mills.

millennium. A thousand years. Some interpret Revelation 20:4–6 to mean that Christ and his followers will reign on earth for a thousand years.

millstone. See **mill.**

minister. 1. To help or serve (Mark 10:45). **2.** Helper or servant (Acts 13:5); especially, someone who helps others in religious work (Colossians 1:23).

miracle. Some event made possible by the power of God, and intended as a sign or revelation of God.

mire. Thick mud (Jeremiah 38:6).

Miriam (mir′i əm). Older sister of Aaron and Moses. She helped to save Moses' life when he was a baby. As a grownup she left Egypt with her brothers and led the women of Israel in singing praises when God helped them to escape across the sea. (Exodus 15:20.)

mite (Hebrew coin)

mite. Smallest, least valuable copper coin in New Testament times; 1/20 to 1/80 of a day's wages.

mitre. Turban worn by a high priest (Exodus 28:4).

Mizpah, Mizpeh (miz′pə). Name (similar in meaning to "Point Lookout" or "Lookout Mountain") of several places; these two were most important: **1.** Place east of the Jordan River where Jacob and his father-in-law Laban made peace after their quarrel (Genesis 31:49). The judge Jephthah later camped there. No one knows exactly where in Jordan this Mizpah was. **2.** City belonging to the tribe of Benjamin (1 Samuel 7:5), a few miles north of Jerusalem (now in Jordan). It was an impor-

tant religious, military, and political center. There Samuel led the Israelites to promise again to worship the true God. For a time after Jerusalem was destroyed in 587 B.C., Mizpah was the capital of the Babylonian province of Judah.

Moab (mō′ab), **Moabites** (mō′ə bīts). Nation that lived east of the Dead Sea. Their main territory was the southern half of this area, but at times they ruled the northern half also. The Moabites tried to block the Israelites from entering Canaan, but do not seem to have fought them as other tribes did. During the times of the judges, Moab was sometimes friendly to Israel, sometimes not. Ruth was a Moabitess, and her great-grandson David sent his family to Moab for protection. During most of the times of the kings, Moab fought against Israel and Judah.

mock. To make fun of.

Molech, Moloch (mō′lək). God of the Ammonites; same as **Milcom.** He was worshiped with human sacrifices.

molten image. Idol made by pouring hot metal into a cast or mold.

moneychanger, money-changer. Man who swapped any kind of money for the special silver coins that must

priest wearing mitre

be used to pay the Temple tax in New Testament times; same as **changer.** For this service he charged a fee—sometimes a large one.

monotheism. Belief that there is only one God.

Mordecai (môr′də kī). Jewish official in the Persian court; cousin and guardian of Esther (Esther 2:5). With Esther's help he foiled a wicked plot against the Jews, and received high honors.

moreover. Besides; also.

Moriah (mō rī′ə). Rocky hilltop where Abraham started to sacrifice Isaac, and where the Temple in Jerusalem was later built. A Moslem shrine stands on Mount Moriah today.

morrow. Next day.

mortify. To put to death; used as a figure of speech for forgetting about, or making unimportant (Romans 8:13; Colossians 3:5).

Moses (mō′ziz). Great leader of the Hebrews; most important Old Testament character. When Moses was born to Amram and Jochebed, his people were slaves in Egypt. With the help of his sister Miriam and an Egyptian princess, he was saved from death and grew up in the royal palace. There he was well educated. As a grown-up he killed an overseer who was mistreating a Hebrew slave, and had to run for his life to Midian. Many years later, God told him to go back to Egypt and lead the Israelites to freedom. At last the Hebrews were set free, but then the Egyptian king changed his mind and tried to recapture them. His army was drowned in the sea, and Moses and the Israelites escaped. For forty years Moses led his people through the wilderness. The most important work he did during this period was to teach and explain God's laws. He made

Aaron the first high priest and directed the making of the tabernacle. Just before the Hebrews entered the Promised Land, Moses announced that Joshua was the new leader. Then he climbed Mount Nebo and died there. Moses is mentioned more often in the New Testament than is any other Old Testament character. (See Exodus, Leviticus, Numbers, Deuteronomy.)

most High. Name for God (Acts 7:48).

most holy place. Innermost room of the tabernacle or the Temple; same as **holy of holies, holiest,** and **oracle** (definition **1**). In it was the ark of the covenant. Only the high priest could enter it, and he only once a year.

mote. Speck; bit of straw.

mourn. To be sad or show sorrow. The Hebrews considered it as important to mourn a dead person properly as to bury him properly. Therefore, they often hired professional mourners (Mark 5:38–40).

mule. Favorite riding animal for kings and noblemen.

multitude. Many persons or things; crowd.

murmur. To complain (Exodus 15:24).

murrain. Cattle disease.

must needs. To have to.

myrrh. Fragrant gum from several types of shrubs, used in perfume. It was sometimes prepared in solid, sometimes in liquid form. Myrrh made up part of the oil for anointing priests, and was one of the Wise Men's gifts to little Jesus.

Mysia (mish′i ə). Northwestern part of Asia Minor (now in Turkey), through which Paul passed without stopping to preach (Acts 16:6–11).

mystery. Something known to God and those to whom God wishes to tell it (Luke 8:10); not just any secret.

Naaman (nā′ə mən). Syrian army commander who was healed of leprosy by the prophet Elisha (2 Kings 5).

Nabal (nā′bəl). Wealthy owner of sheep and goats who rudely refused David's request for permission to attend his shearing festival, after David's men had protected his flocks from harm (1 Samuel 25).

Naboth (nā′bəth). Owner of a vineyard in Jezreel who was killed by Queen Jezebel so that King Ahab could get his land (1 Kings 21).

Nahor (nā′hôr). Family name in Abraham's tribe. His grandfather and brother bore that name (Genesis 11:24–26). So did a city where many of his relatives lived (Genesis 24:10).

Nahum (nā′əm). **1.** Prophet of Judah, the Southern Kingdom, about 633–612 B.C. He might have prophesied in the Temple at Jerusalem, but almost nothing is known about him. **2.** Old Testament book of the Minor Prophets, containing a fierce poem in which Nahum vividly described the fall of the great and wicked city of Nineveh. In that turning point of world events, the prophet could see that God was working out his own purposes.

Nain (nān). Town in Galilee where Jesus brought back to life a widow's only son. Today the Israeli village —about 5 miles southeast of Nazareth—is called Nein.

name. Often means who someone really is, not just what he is called. To know and praise the name of God means to know and praise God himself (Psalm 9:2,10). To "name the name of Christ" means to be the follower of Christ (2 Timothy 2:19).

Naomi (nā ō′mi). Jewish widow who returned to Bethlehem with her Moabite daughter-in-law Ruth. "Naomi" means lovely or pleasant (Ruth 1–4).

Naphtali (naf′tə lī). Son of Jacob; tribe of Israel occupying territory northwest of the Sea of Galilee.

napkin. Any small piece of cloth (John 11:44).

nard

nard. Expensive, fragrant ointment made from a plant that grows in India; same as **spikenard**.

Nathan (nā′thən). Name of several Old Testament men, of whom the best-known was a prophet at King David's court (2 Samuel 7;12). He told the king what God commanded him to say, even though it was sometimes not what the king wanted to hear.

Nathanael (nə than′i əl). Friend of Philip the disciple who lived in Cana and was brought by Philip to Jesus. He became one of Jesus' followers also. Many people think he was the same man as **Bartholo-**

mew, one of Jesus' twelve apostles. (John 1:45.)

nativity. Birth; especially, the birth of Jesus.

naughty. Very bad or worthless; not just improper or prankish (Proverbs 6:12).

nay. No.

Nazarene (naz′ə rēn). **1.** Person who was born or grew up in Nazareth (Matthew 2:23). **2.** Follower of Jesus of Nazareth (Acts 24:5).

Nazareth (naz′ə rith). Town in Galilee, about halfway between the Mediterranean Sea and the southern tip of the Sea of Galilee; home of Joseph, Mary, and Jesus. It was not mentioned in the Old Testament; perhaps this is why some people did not expect the Christ to come from there (John 1:46). In New Testament times it was a small village, off the main highways, with hills on three sides. There Jesus and his half brothers and sisters grew up. Of the many Nazareth places shown to tourists in Israel today, the village well is the only one which might really have been known and used by Jesus' family.

Nazarite, Nazirite (naz′ə rīt). Person who made a special pledge to give himself to the Lord's service, and showed this dedication by refusing to cut his hair or to drink wine (Numbers 6; Judges 13).

Neapolis (nē ap′ə lis). Seaport of Philippi, at which Paul landed in Macedonia (Acts 16:11); now Kaválla in northeastern Greece.

Nebo (nē′bō). Mountain about 12 miles east of the mouth of the Jordan River, where Moses saw the Promised Land before he died. It is 2,740 feet above sea level, and 4,030 higher than the nearby valleys. From one of its peaks (probably also called **Pisgah**) a person

can, on a clear day, see Mount Hermon—115 miles to the north. Jordanians today call Nebo Jabal an Nabā.

Nebuchadnezzar (neb′ə kəd nez′ər *or* neb′yoo kəd nez′ər). Powerful king of Babylonia about 605–562 B.C. He conquered Judah, the Southern Kingdom, and led many of its people into captivity (2 Kings 24–25). The book of Jeremiah uses a more accurate form of his name: Nebuchadrezzar. But the other spelling is more often used.

Nebuzaradan (neb′ə zə rā′dən). Important official of King Nebuchadnezzar who took charge of destroying Jerusalem in 587 B.C. (2 Kings 25:8).

Necho, Nechoh, Neco (nē′kō). King of Egypt who killed in battle King Josiah of Judah, the Southern Kingdom. Soon after, he threw young King Jehoahaz into prison and placed Jehoiakim on the throne (2 Kings 23:29–35).

neesings. Sneezings.

Negeb (neg′eb), **Negev** (neg′ev). Area southwest of the Dead Sea; often called "the **south.**" It was a fairly fertile section in Bible times. In the centuries since, it has lost most of its vegetation and is today almost a desert. Modern Israelis are using

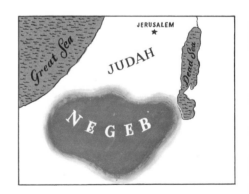

irrigation to make the Negeb fruitful again.

Nehemiah (nē'ə mī'ə). **1.** Jewish court official of King Artaxerxes I of Persia who returned to his ancestors' home and rebuilt the walls of Jerusalem. He was one of the most clever and hardworking men of Bible times, overcoming many obstacles in order to finish his hard job. He served as Persian governor of Jerusalem and nearby areas for many years. **2.** Old Testament book of History. Chapters 1–6 tell the exciting story of Nehemiah's return to Jerusalem and the rebuilding of the walls. Chapters 7–13 contain other material—some about Nehemiah, some about Ezra. Nehemiah himself wrote at least part of the book, for it reads like a diary.

nephew. Male descendant, grandson (1 Timothy 5:4).

mentioned several places in the Bible; eternal home of those who trust in God.

new moon. Special Hebrew religious festival on the day a new moon appeared. It was like an especially important sabbath day. The date for the Passover was figured in relation to the new moon.

New Testament. 1. New covenant made between God and man through Jesus Christ (1 Corinthians 11:25; Hebrews 9:15). **2.** Second part of the Bible; 27 books that tell about Jesus Christ and the new covenant he brought between God and man.

Nicodemus (nik ə dē'məs). Jewish ruler and teacher in Jerusalem who secretly talked with Jesus one night and later seems to have become a secret follower of his (John 3:1–21).

nigh. Near.

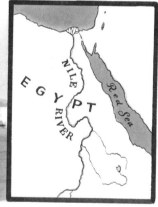

Nile River

nether. Lower or under.

Nethinim (neth'ə nim), **Nethinims** (neth'ə nimz). Servants of the priests and Levites in the Temple.

new birth. What happens when someone is **born again;** same as **regeneration.**

New Jerusalem (nyōo' jə rōo'sə ləm). Capital city of God's new creation,

Nile (nīl). Great river whose waters bring life to Egypt—such an important stream that the Hebrew word for it simply means "the **river**" (Exodus 2:5).

Nineveh, Nineve (nin'ə və). Greatest capital of Assyria. It lay on the Tigris River, in what is now northern Iraq. In 612 B.C. an unexpected flood weakened Nineveh's mud-brick walls, and helped Assyria's enemies to capture and completely destroy it. A modern village atop one of the mounds of ruins is a reminder of the man whom God sent to preach to Nineveh. The village is named Nebi Yunus —"Prophet Jonah."

Nisan (nī′zan). First month of the Hebrew year—March-April, beginning with the new moon in March.

Noah, Noe (nō′ə). Man of early Old Testament times who built an ark at God's instruction in order to escape a great flood. The Bible calls him the only really good man of his times (Genesis 5–9).

noise. To make known (Mark 2:1).

noisome. Harmful; dangerous; deadly (Psalm 91:3).

notwithstanding. In spite of that (Luke 10:11).

no wise. No way (Luke 13:11).

Numbers (num′bərz). Fourth book of the Old Testament, and of the section called Law. Besides many laws, it also includes much history. The first part tells what happened at Mount Sinai. Then comes the story of the twelve spies and the Israelites' refusal to enter the Promised Land. Next are stories about the forty years of wandering in the desert. The book ends as the Israelites are again near the border of the Promised Land. The title refers to a census, or numbering of the people, that Moses directed.

oath. Serious promise, sworn in God's name, that a person will or will not do a certain thing; often includes a request that God will punish the person if he breaks his promise: "May the Lord do so to me and more also."

Obadiah (ō′bə dī′ə). **1.** Governor of King Ahab's household (1 Kings 18:3). Unlike his master, he faithfully worshiped the Lord God. **2.** Prophet who lived about 587 B.C. Almost nothing is known about him. **3.** Old Testament book of the Minor Prophets; shortest book of the Old Testament. The prophet Obadiah predicted that the Edomites would be punished because they had long been the Hebrews' enemies, and, especially, because they had joined with the Babylonians in conquering Jerusalem.

Obed (ō′bid). Son of Boaz and Ruth; grandfather of King David (Ruth 4:17).

obeisance. Act of deep respect; bow or curtsy.

oblation. Sacrifice.

occasion. Cause or reason; especially, cause for taking some action against a person (Daniel 6:4).

occupy. To trade or have business dealings (Luke 19:13).

of. Besides the usual definitions, often means: **1.** From (Exodus 22:14; Acts 3:2,5). **2.** For (Daniel 2:47; Acts 10:34). **3.** By (1 Chronicles 2:18; Matthew 4:1). **4.** About (Daniel 5:14; Mark 1:30). **5.** With (2 Samuel 19:32; Matthew 18:23). **6.** At (2 Samuel 19:42; Acts 21:32). **7.** Through (Matthew 1:22; 2:15). **8.** On (Hebrews 10:34; Revelation 8:13).

offend. Besides the usual definitions, means to make someone stumble —that is, fall into sin (Matthew 18:6).

offering. **1.** Similar to **sacrifice** (Leviticus 1:2). **2.** Gift of money or other possessions for God's work—

such as building the tabernacle (Exodus 35:5) or helping the poor (Acts 24:17).

offspring. Child or children; the young of animals.

Og (äg). Giant king of Bashan who fought against the Israelites on their way into the Promised Land (Numbers 21:33).

Oholiab (ō hō'li ab). Bezaleel's helper in making the ark of the covenant and other holy objects in the tabernacle; same as **Aholiab** (Exodus 31:6).

oil. Nearly always means olive oil, which was considered one of the necessities of life in Bible times. It was used as cooking fat; hair dressing, and similar aids to good looks; fuel for lamps; and medicine for wounds. It was also used to anoint kings and priests and to mix with sacrifices.

ointment. Oil used for anointing, often mixed with perfume.

Old Testament. 1. Covenant God made with Abraham and his descendants (2 Corinthians 3:14). The new testament or covenant is the one God makes with everyone who gives himself to Jesus Christ. **2.** First part of the Bible: 39 books that tell about the first covenant God made, and the people with whom he made it.

Olives, Mount of (mount' əv äl'ivz). Long ridge just east of Jerusalem (now in Jordan); same as **Olivet.** Bethany was on the eastern side of it, Gethsemane on the western side, and Bethphage probably somewhere near the crest.

Olivet (äl'ə vit). Same as **"Olives, Mount of."**

Omega (ō mē'gə or ō mā'gə). See **Alpha and Omega.**

omer. Dry measure; a little more than 2 quarts.

omnipotent. Having all power (Revelation 19:6).

Omri (äm'rī). Powerful king of Israel, the Northern Kingdom, about 880–869 B.C. He had to win a civil war to be king, but became one of Israel's strongest rulers. More than a hundred years after his death, Israel was still sometimes called "the land of Omri." He was succeeded by his wicked son Ahab (1 Kings 16:16).

Onesimus (ō nes'ə məs). Runaway slave who met Paul while Paul was a prisoner, became a Christian, and returned to his master, carrying the letter we call the book of Philemon.

on high. 1. Above (Isaiah 40:26). **2.** In heaven (Hebrews 1:3).

only begotten. One of a kind; the only one; unique.

on this wise. Like this (Matthew 1:18).

open. Sometimes means to explain (Luke 24:32; Acts 17:3).

oracle. 1. Same as **most holy place** (1 Kings 6:23). **2.** Special message from God (Romans 3:2).

ordain. 1. To cause to be; to make to happen (Psalm 8:2). **2.** To set apart as a special worker for God (1 Timothy 2:7).

ordinance. Law, command, or order (Exodus 12:24); especially, baptism or the Lord's Supper, since Jesus commanded his followers to perform these acts.

or ever. Before (Daniel 6:24).

organ. Type of musical instrument—probably a silver flute or pipe (Psalm 150:4); not an organ as known today.

Ornan (ôr'nan). Same as **Araunah.**

Orpah (ôr'pə). Naomi's daughter-in-law who finally returned to her own people in the land of Moab.

Oshea (ō shē'ə). Same as **Joshua.**

ouches. Settings for precious stones (Exodus 39:6).

ought. Anything (John 4:33).

outwent. Outran (Mark 6:33).

clay oven

oven. Jar-like clay cylinder, built up about 2 or 3 feet wide on a pebble floor. A fire, often of dried grass (Matthew 6:30), was built inside. When the oven was hot enough, coals and ashes were swept away and flat pancake-like bread was slapped onto the sides or the pebble floor to bake.

over against. Opposite or in front of.

overcharge. To overload or weigh down (2 Corinthians 2:5).

overdrive. To drive too hard (Genesis 33:13).

overlive. To outlive (Joshua 24:31).

Paddan-aram (pad ən ar əm), **Padan-aram** (pā′dən ar′əm). Area around Haran where Abraham once lived, and where many of his relatives stayed (now in southeast central Turkey).

Palestina (pal′əs tē′nə). Same as **Philistia** (Exodus 15:14; Isaiah 14:29, 31).

Palestine (pal′əs tīn). **1.** Same as **Philistia** (Joel 3:4). **2.** Name (not used with that meaning in the Bible) for the area in which most of the events described in the Bible took place; same as the **Holy Land.** Palestine includes the narrow strip of land between the Mediterranean Sea and the Sea of Galilee, Jordan River, and Dead Sea; also, some of the territory east of the Jordan. This area is now mainly divided between Jordan and Israel, with small parts of it in Syria, Lebanon, and the Gaza Strip. Israel is still called Occupied Palestine by Arab countries.

palsy. Paralysis (Mark 2:4); not just an uncontrollable shaking.

Paphos (pā′fəs). Seaport on the southwestern coast of Cyprus, where Paul and Barnabas preached on their first missionary journey. It was then the Roman capital of Cyprus.

parable (par′ə b'l). Brief story that teaches a truth. The word means comparison; in a parable, one thing is compared to another for teaching purposes. The best-known parables are those Jesus told.

Paraclete (par′ə klēt). Name for the **Holy Spirit.** It means "someone that you call to your side"—that is, someone who helps and encourages you.

Paradise (par′ə dīs). Name for **heaven.** It means garden or park, because heaven was thought of as being like the Garden of Eden.

Paran (par′ən). Desert area southwest of the Dead Sea in which the Israelites wandered for many years; now mainly in Israel.

parchments. Animal skins prepared so that they can be written on (2 Timothy 4:13).

part. To separate or divide up (Luke 23:34; 24:51).

pass. Besides the usual meanings, sometimes means to surpass, go beyond, or be greater than (Ephesians 3:19; Philippians 4:7).

passage. 1. Ford (Judges 12:5). 2. Mountain pass (1 Samuel 14:4).

passion. Jesus' sufferings and death (Acts 1:3); also, used as adjective to describe any drama, music, or worship service that tells about or recalls these events.

Passover (pas'ō'vər). One of the Hebrews' most important festivals, celebrated in the spring each year; same as **"Unleavened Bread, Feast of,"** and also called **Easter** in some translations of Acts 12:4. The name Passover comes from the fact that death passed over each Israelite home in Egypt which was marked on its doorposts with the blood of the lamb eaten in the feast. Passover helped the Hebrews to remember that God had freed them from slavery. Exact details of the observance varied according to time and place. In Jesus' time, all who could do so observed the Passover in Jerusalem. The lamb was killed in the Temple, brought back and roasted whole, and served with unleavened bread (made without yeast), bitter herbs (to remind of bitter slavery), a paste made of fruits and nuts (to remind of the mortar used with bricks in Egypt), and wine. A son in each family asked the question, "Why is this night different from all other nights?" Then the story of the first Passover was retold.

pastor. 1. Shepherd (Jeremiah 2:8). 2. Leader of a church, who should care for the members as tenderly as a shepherd cares for his sheep (Ephesians 4:11).

Pastoral Epistles, Pastoral Letters. Name given to 1 Timothy, 2 Timothy, and Titus, since they give advice to young pastors from an older one.

patience. Steadfastness; "stick-to-itiveness" (James 5:11).

Patmos (pat'məs). Small, rocky island in the Aegean Sea, to which John was exiled as punishment, and on which he had the visions described in Revelation; now belongs to Greece.

patriarchs. 1. Abraham, Isaac, and Jacob, the forefathers of the Hebrew people (Hebrews 7:4). 2. Jacob's sons or grandsons, forefathers of the twelve tribes of Israel (Acts 7:8–9). 3. All great leaders of God's people in Old Testament times (Acts 2:29).

Paul (pôl). Jewish persecutor of Christians who became the greatest Christian leader of his time, and perhaps of all times. He was born in Tarsus (now in south central Turkey) about A.D. 5, and given the Jewish name **Saul** and the Greek name Paul. His family was probably wealthy and important to some degree. A strict Pharisee, he studied with the best teachers in Jerusalem. In the years after the resurrection, he began to persecute Christians because he thought they were turning people away from true faith in God. On the way to imprison Christians in Damascus, he had a vision of the risen Christ, whom he ever after followed faithfully. Some years later, Barnabas brought him to Antioch in Syria as a fellow pastor. From there the two left on a first missionary journey. They visited Cyprus and what are now several parts of Turkey—preaching, teaching, healing, and winning many, but suffering many hardships. Later Paul and Silas made a longer trip, covering much of what are now Turkey and Greece. A third trip included some of these and other areas. Then Paul was arrested on false charges in Jerusalem, held in prison for two years at Caesarea, and sent to Rome for further trial. On the way he was shipwrecked, but finally arrived safely. The Bible does not clearly say, but it seems that Paul was set free, made several more missionary trips, and finally was put into prison again. Probably he was beheaded at Rome about A.D. 68. His importance for Christianity is shown by these facts (among many others): He wrote more books of the New Testament than any other person. More than half of the book of Acts tells about his life and work.

Pauline Epistles (pôl'ēn i pis''lz), **Pauline Letters** (pôl'ēn let'ərz), **Paul's Epistles.** Same as **Paul's Letters.**

Paul's Letters. Section of New Testament books: Romans, 1 and 2 Corinthians, Galatians, Ephesians, Philippians, Colossians, 1 and 2 Thessalonians, 1 and 2 Timothy, Titus, and Philemon. Each is named after the person or persons to whom Paul wrote it.

Paulus, Sergius (sûr'ji əs pôl'əs). Roman **proconsul** of Cyprus who became one of the first new believers on Paul's first missionary journey (Acts 13:7–12).

peace. To "hold one's peace" means to keep quiet or make no disturbance (Mark 3:4).

peace offering. Sacrifice of some animal, made as a way of thanking God, of keeping a promise to God, or of expressing love for God. Part of the animal was eaten by the priests. The rest was eaten near the altar by the person who offered it. He often shared this special holy meal with friends.

peculiar. One's very own; personal

(Psalm 135:4).

Pelethites (pel'ə thīts). See **Cherethites and Pelethites.**

pence. Plural of **penny** or **denarius;** denarii.

Peniel (pə nī'əl *or* pen'i əl). Same as **Penuel.**

penny. Same as **denarius** (Mark 12:15). The denarius was a valuable silver coin, worth enough to pay a man for a day's work. The word "penny," used in some translations, does not indicate the correct value.

Pentateuch (pen'tə tōōk *or* pen'tə-tyōōk). "Five Books"—the first five books of the Bible.

Pentecost (pen'ti kôst). **1.** Same as **Weeks, Feast of.** "Pentecost" means fiftieth, because this feast came on the fiftieth day after Passover (Acts 20:16). **2.** First Pentecost after the resurrection, when the Holy Spirit came to Jesus' followers, as he had promised (Acts 2:1).

Penuel (pi nōō'əl *or* pen'yoo əl). Place on the Jabbok River, east of the Jordan, where Jacob had an unusual experience with God one night; same as **Peniel.** Both names mean face of God. No one knows exactly where Penuel was.

penury. Condition of being very poor and in great need.

people of God, people of the Lord. Same as **Chosen People.** The New Testament shows that God's people are the ones who do his will by accepting Jesus Christ as Lord and Saviour. Christians are called the people of God (1 Peter 2:10).

peradventure. Perhaps.

perceive. To realize; to take in; to "catch on."

perdition. Death; complete and everlasting destruction.

Perea (pə rē'ə). Name given in New Testament times to the area east of the Jordan River. Jesus made his last trip to Jerusalem through Perea.

perfect. Often means, not necessarily without faults or mistakes, but complete; having all the parts needed; not lacking anything (Luke 1:3; Matthew 5:48).

Perga (pûr′gə). Important city in Pamphylia, a Roman province (now in southeastern Turkey). Here John Mark left Paul and Barnabas on their first missionary journey.

peril. Danger.

perish. 1. To die (Esther 4:16). 2. To be destroyed (2 Samuel 1:27). 3. To be lost from God and salvation (John 3:16).

Perizzites (per′ə zīts). One of the tribes driven out of Canaan by the Israelites. No one knows much about them.

persecute. To keep on treating someone in a mean or cruel way, especially because he holds certain beliefs.

perseverance. Continued efforts; "stick-to-it-iveness."

Persia (pûr′zhə), **Persians** (pûr′zhənz). Nation that ruled what is now Iran, plus (at times) many other areas. Persia conquered Babylonia in 539 B.C., and thus also took over the Jews who lived in Babylonia and those still in and near Jerusalem. It was a Persian king who first allowed Jews to return from Babylonia; another who married Esther; another who sent Nehemiah to rebuild the walls. Persia was conquered by Alexander the Great in 331 B.C. but later became a nation again.

person. Besides the usual meanings, has three others—two found in the Bible, the third used in discussing biblical subjects: **1.** To "accept the person" of someone means to let him come near in friendship, as a king might do for someone who enters his court begging for help (Malachi 1:8; Luke 20:21). **2.** To "regard the person" or "respect the person" of someone means to make him a favorite in a way that is unfair to others (Leviticus 19:15; Acts 10:34; James 2:9). **3.** Father, Son, and Holy Spirit are spoken of as the three "persons" of God, or the three ways God has made himself personally known to men; see **Trinity.**

persuaded. Besides the usual definition means to be absolutely sure (Romans 8:38).

pertain. To belong to or be concerned with.

perverse. Continuing stubbornly to do what is wrong or harmful; often literally means twisted out of proper shape.

pestilence. Epidemic of a dangerous disease.

Peter (pē′tər). **1.** Leading disciple among Jesus' original twelve; outstanding leader among early Christians. His original name was **Simon, Simeon,** or **Symeon.** Jesus gave him his new name: in its Aramaic form, **Cephas;** in its Greek form, Peter. Both mean rock. Peter was not really steady like a rock at first, but Jesus saw, in him and in his faith, the possibility for strong leadership. Peter's original hometown was Beth-saida (John 1:44). He and his brother Andrew became partners with James and John in the fishing business at Capernaum (Mark 1:21,29; Luke 5:10). Andrew first brought Peter to Jesus; later, Jesus called both to become special disciples. During the years that the twelve learned from Jesus, Peter was most often their spokesman. When Jesus was captured, Peter claimed that he did not even know who Jesus was. After the resurrection Jesus again asked Peter to serve him. With new courage

Peter became the Christians' leader. He preached to thousands in Jerusalem, refused to stop when jailed and threatened, and later traveled to other places as a missionary—Samaria, Lydda, Joppa, Caesarea, and probably places far more distant. An early Christian historian says that Peter was finally crucified head downward. **2.** Two New Testament books in the section called General Letters: 1 Peter and 2 Peter. First Peter was written to Christians in parts of Asia Minor. It points out that Christians are now God's special people and should behave as such. It warns that persecution should come as no surprise, and should be faced bravely. Second Peter explains that all of God's promises can be depended upon—that God's judgment and the end of the world will, indeed, come in God's own good time.

petition. Request.

Pharaoh (fer′ō *or* fer′i ō). Title of the king of Egypt, sometimes used as if it were a name.

Pharisees (far′ə sēz). Important Jewish religious and political party in Jesus' time. Pharisees at first kept up the tradition of the prophets, while Sadducees kept up the tradition of the priests. Later, the Pharisees placed highest importance on keeping the law. They invented many petty rules, intended to make it more nearly possible to obey every one of the rules in the Old Testament. Many Pharisees were sincere about their religion. Others, however, made a great show of going through all the motions of religion, but actually forgot about true worship.

Phebe (fē′bi). Same as **Phoebe.**

Phenice (fə nī′si). 1. Same as **Phoenix** (Acts 27:12). 2. Same as **Phoe-**

nicia (Acts 11:19; 15:3).

Phenicia (fə nish′ə *or* fə nē′shə). Same as **Phoenicia** (Acts 21:2).

Philemon (fī lē′mən *or* fə lē′mən). **1.** Wealthy Christian in Colossae who was probably a leader of the church there and owner of the runaway slave Onesimus. **2.** New Testament book; the shortest of Paul's letters. Paul sent Onesimus back with the letter, asking that he be received as a brother. The little note has been called one of the most beautiful and skilful ever written.

Philip (fil′ip). **1.** One of the Herods who ruled (with the title of tetrarch) the area north and east of the Sea of Galilee (Luke 3:1). **2.** Another Herod who was the first husband of Herodias (Mark 6:17). **3.** One of Jesus' twelve apostles (Mark 3:18). He brought his friend Nathanael to Jesus also. His hometown was Beth-saida. From his conversations with Jesus, some people have guessed that Philip was a bit slow to understand who Jesus was and what kind of work he was doing. **4.** One of seven Jerusalem Christians chosen to help the apostles, especially with caring for the poor (Acts 6:5). Later he preached to Samaritans and to an Ethiopian court official. His home was Caesarea, where he lived with four unmarried daughters who were also active Christian workers.

Philippi (fil′ə pī). Important city and Roman colony in Macedonia where Paul preached, converted Lydia and others, was thrown into jail, and converted the jailer and his family. The ruins of Philippi now lie in northeastern Greece.

Philippians (fi lip′i ənz). New Testament book; one of Paul's letters. The church at Philippi seems to have been Paul's favorite, and his letter to those Christians has a happy, friendly tone not matched in anything else he wrote. The Philippians had sent Paul a message and help (probably money) while he was in prison. He wrote to thank them, to tell them how he was getting along and what he hoped to do in the future, and to urge them to behave as Christians should.

Philistia (fə lis'ti ə), **Philistines** (fə lis'-tinz *or* fil'ə stēnz *or* fil'ə stīnz), **Philistim** (fə lis'tim). Tribe that ruled several city-states along the Mediterranean seacoast, from Joppa to below Gaza (now in Israel and the Gaza Strip; the words **Palestina** and **Palestine** were also sometimes used to mean this area). The Philistines were a sort of pirate tribe that finally settled down. They mined iron and made it into armor and weapons which they knew well how to use. During the times of the judges, King Saul, and King David, the Philistines were among the Israelites' most dangerous enemies. David defeated them so soundly that they were never quite so strong again.

Phoebe (fē'bi). Important woman in the church at Cenchre-ae, the seaport of Corinth, who carried one of Paul's letters; same as **Phebe** (Romans 16:1).

Phoenicia (fə nish'ə *or* fə nē'shə), **Phoenicians** (fə nish'ənz *or* fə nē'shənz). Tribe that lived along the Mediterranean seacoast near Galilee and on to the north (now in Israel and Lebanon; this area was also sometimes called **Phenicia** or **Phenice**). They were great sailors and traders, especially in fine red, blue, and purple dyes made from a certain type of sea snail. Tyre and Sidon were among the Phoenicians' strong city-states.

Phoenix (fē'niks). Harbor in southern Crete that Paul's ship tried in vain to reach on its way to Rome; same as **Phenice** (in Acts 27:12).

Phrygia (frij'i ə). Area in Asia Minor (now southwest central Turkey) that included the Galatian cities where Paul started churches, and also Colossae and nearby cities.

arm phylactery (see also frontlets)

phylacteries. Small boxes containing Old Testament verses that Jews wore on their foreheads and left arms while praying. The verses were Exodus 13:1–10, 11–16; Deuteronomy 6:4–9; 11:13–21. The forehead phylacteries were sometimes called **frontlets**. (See also **mezuzah**.) Jesus accused some people of tying on phylacteries with broader leather straps than were needed, so as to call attention to the fact that they were praying.

piece of money. 1. Quantity of silver measured by weight—not by coins, which were unknown till later Old Testament times. No one knows exactly what the weight was (Genesis 33:19). **2.** Large silver coin of New Testament times, equal to four days' wages, and enough to pay the Temple tax for two men (Matthew 17:27).

piece of silver. 1. Much the same as **piece of money,** definition **1,** although the weight may not have been the same. **2.** Same as **denarius** (Luke 15:8). **3.** Same as **piece of money,** definition **2** (Matthew 26:15).

Pilate, Pontius (pän'shəs pī'lət *or* pän'ti əs pī'lət). Roman procurator or governor of Judea who condemned Jesus to death. He ruled A.D. 26–36. One early historian says Pilate committed so many crimes that the Romans finally had to replace him.

Pisgah (piz'gə). See **Nebo**.

pit. Sometimes used as a word for **hell**, definition **1** (Numbers 16:30, 33; Job 17:16; 33:28,30).

pitch. Black, tar-like fluid.

pitiful. Showing pity or mercy (1 Peter 3:8).

pity. Sympathy; mercy; feeling of being sorry for; often used in the phrases, "to have pity upon," or "to take pity upon."

plague. Epidemic of deadly disease, or other form of disaster; especially the disasters suffered by the Egyptians when their king refused to free the Israelites.

plain. Besides the usual meanings, has these two others: **1.** Same as **Arabah** (Deuteronomy 2:8). **2.** Same as **Shephelah** (Obadiah 19).

pledge. Piece of personal property (such as a ring or outer robe) given to someone as proof that a debt will be paid (Job 24:3), or that some other promise will be kept (Genesis 38:17–18), or that the person giving the object is in good health and circumstances (1 Samuel 17:18).

plenteous. Plentiful.

ploughshare, plowshare. Cutting blade of a plow.

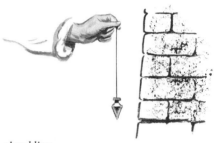

plumbline

plumbline, plummet. Weight (of metal, stone, or clay) hanging free on a line to test the straightness of a wall; used as a figure of speech for the way God tests people (Amos 7:7–8).

Poetry. Section of Old Testament books, including Job, Psalms, Proverbs, Ecclesiastes, and Song of Solomon. Actually, much of Ecclesiastes and parts of Job are prose. There is much poetry in other Bible books. One third of the Old Testament is written in poetry, and several verses of the New Testament. Bible poetry rarely rhymes,

farmer with a ploughshare

even in the original languages, but it does have strong rhythms.

pollute. To make unclean, or break a taboo; see **clean.**

pomegranate

pomegranate. Fruit that looks like a hard, reddish orange; its pulp is red, juicy, and delicious, but full of seeds. Pomegranates grow on small, shrublike trees.

ponder. To think about deeply and carefully.

possessed. In the power of; under the control of; usually used to describe someone whose mind was troubled by an evil spirit.

potentate. Person having great power.

Potiphar (pät′ə fər). Egyptian official who bought Joseph as a slave (Genesis 37:36).

potsherd. Piece of broken pottery; same as **sherd** or **shard.** When archaeologists dig out biblical cities, potsherds often give them the best clues to who lived there, and when.

pottage. Thick vegetable soup, usually made with **lentils.**

pound. 1. Measure of weight—about 1-1/4 pound (Ezra 2:69). **2.** Measure of weight—about 3/4 pound (John 12:3). **3.** Amount of money—about 100 days' wages (Luke 19:13).

Praetorium (prē tōr′i əm). Some area of a Roman palace—either a judg-

ment hall, courtyard, or soldiers' barracks (Mark 15:16).

praise. 1. To worship (Psalm 9:1). **2.** To say good things about (Proverbs 27:2).

pray. 1. To talk with God; to worship God, thank him, and ask things of him (Matthew 5:44). **2.** To ask or beg for something (Genesis 18:4).

preacher, the. See **Koheleth.**

precept. Command; rule.

predestinate. To decide or choose beforehand (Romans 8:29–30).

pre-eminence. First place; most outstanding rank.

prefer. To promote; to put in a higher place (Daniel 6:3).

preparation. Besides the usual definitions, means Friday, the day when special preparation for the sabbath was made (Mark 15:42); or the day before the Passover, when even more preparing was done (John 19:14).

presbyter (prez′bi tər). Same as **elder;** "presbytery" means a group of older leaders (1 Timothy 4:14).

presently. Immediately; at once (Proverbs 12:16).

preserve. To keep; to protect (Deuteronomy 6:24).

press. 1. Same as **wine vat** or **wine press** (Isaiah 16:10). **2.** Crowd (Luke 19:3). **3.** To push or force (Luke 6:38; Philippians 3:14).

prevail. 1. To win or be successful (Lamentations 1:16). **2.** To become more common or widespread than before (Genesis 7:18; 47:20).

prevent. 1. To go before (Psalm 119:147; 1 Thessalonians 4:15). **2.** To receive (Job 3:12).

pricks. Same as **goad.**

priest. Someone who speaks to God, or has to do with God, in behalf of others. In the Hebrew religion, priests took charge of public worship services, prepared sacrifices, and led in special prayers. Usually part of the sacrifices went to feed them and their families, so that they could spend their time in religious duties. See also **high priest** and **Levites.**

principality, principalities. Spirits. Sometimes applied to angelic beings (Ephesians 3:10) and sometimes to evil powers (Romans 8:38).

Prisca (pris′kə), **Priscilla** (pri sil′ə). Aquila's wife and co-worker.

privily. Secretly (Matthew 2:7).

privy to. Secretly informed about (Acts 5:2).

proclaim. To announce.

proclamation. Public announcement.

proconsul. Civil and military governor of a Roman province; same as **deputy.**

procurator. Military and financial official of the Roman Empire; often served as governor of a province.

prodigal. Person who wastes his money recklessly; not a Bible word, but often used to describe the younger son in a story Jesus told (Luke 15:11–32).

profane. To treat something holy as if it were not holy (Acts 24:6).

profess. 1. To make clearly known; to declare openly (1 Timothy 6:12). 2. To claim (Titus 1:16).

Promised Land. Canaan—so called because God promised to give it to Abraham's tribe.

prophecy. 1. Power or act of prophesying (1 Corinthians 13:2). 2. Something spoken or written by a prophet (2 Peter 1:21).

prophesy. 1. To speak for God, or write what God inspires (Amos 7:15). 2. To predict (Mark 7:6).

prophetess. Woman prophet.

prophets. Persons who speak for God. A true prophet's main job was to tell people God's message for the here and now; predicting the future

was only a side line. Prophets were "forth-tellers" more than foretellers. Some prophets, such as Elijah and Elisha, performed many mighty deeds, but did not write down their prophecies. Others wrote many Old Testament books. Five are called Major Prophets: Isaiah through Daniel. Twelve books, from Hosea to Malachi, are called Minor Prophets primarily because their books are short. See these individual book titles in this dictionary; see also **law** and **Writings.**

propitiation. Act that makes possible the forgiveness of sin and a new and close relationship between God and man; what Jesus did for us (1 John 2:2).

proselyte. Gentile who has become a Jew in religion (Acts 2:10).

protest. To insist; to state positively (1 Corinthians 15:31).

prove. 1. To show that something is correct (Acts 24:13). 2. To test (Luke 14:19; John 6:6).

provender. Fodder; food for farm animals.

Proverbs (präv′ərbz). Old Testament book of Poetry. As the name tells, Proverbs contains many short, pithy sayings. It also includes several longer poems—some praising wisdom, spoken of as if it were a wise woman teacher (1:20–33; 3:13–18; 4:1–13); another telling how kings should behave (31:2–9); another describing a good wife and mother (31:10–31). Solomon is mentioned as one of the writers of the book. So are Agur, Lemuel, and others. Probably Proverbs in its complete form was intended as a school textbook for young Jews.

pruning hook. Blade attached to a handle, used to cut off unneeded twigs or branches.

Psalms (sämz). Old Testament book of Poetry; longest book in the

Bible, also the middle book. It includes the longest chapter (119) and the shortest (117, which is also the middle chapter). The Hebrew name of the book means "Praises"; the English name means "Songs Accompanied by Stringed Instruments." Both titles show what Psalms really is: a hymnbook. Its 150 hymns were sung in worship by the Hebrews, and are still sung by Jews and Christians today. David and many others are listed as authors in the titles of the chapters. However, these titles are not really part of the inspired Bible, and were not written till many years after the hymns themselves were. No one knows for sure who wrote the Psalms, or who collected them—first into five smaller hymnbooks (1–41; 42–72; 73–89; 90–106; 107–150), then into one bigger one.

psalter. Same as **Psalms.**

psaltery. 1. Same as **harp** (Psalm 92:3). **2.** Musical instrument similar to a modern zither or dulcimer (Daniel 3).

publican. Tax collector for the Roman government. Since publicans collected money for a foreign conqueror, and since they were often greedy and dishonest, they were fiercely hated.

publish. To announce; to make known (Mark 1:45).

Publius (pub′li əs). Roman official on Malta who welcomed Paul, and whose father Paul healed.

purge. To make pure or clean.

purify. To make pure, clean, or free from taboo; see **clean.**

Purim (poor′im *or* pyoor′im). Jewish festival celebrating the victory of Esther and Mordecai over the wicked plot of Haman. It is unusual among Jewish feasts in being a time of gay and noisy parties, when the story of Esther is acted

out with great glee.

purloin. To steal.

purple. Fine cloth or clothing dyed reddish-purple. It was worn by kings and rich people.

put away. When referring to a wife, means to divorce (Matthew 1:19; 5:31).

Puteoli (pyōō tē′ə li). City on the Bay of Naples in Italy, where Paul landed on his way to Rome; now called Pozzuoli. The old name was probably given to suggest the bad smells at Puteoli, caused by sulphur nearby.

put off. To take off (Exodus 3:5).

quaternion. Squad of four soldiers.

queen of Sheba (kwēn′ əv shē′bə). **queen of the south.** Ruler of the Sabeans, who lived in **Sheba** (the area now known as Yemen) who made a trip of 1,500 miles to visit King Solomon, wishing to find out for herself about his wealth and wisdom.

quick. Alive (Acts 10:42).

quicken. To make alive (Ephesians 2:5).

quit you like men. Act like men; show how manly you are (1 Corinthians 16:13).

quiver. 1. Case for carrying arrows at one's side (Job 39:23). **2.** To tremble (Habakkuk 3:16).

Rabbah (rab′ə), **Rabbath** (rab′əth). Capital city of the Ammonites; now 'Ammān, capital city of Jordan. The Ammonite city was destroyed about 580 B.C. Later, a Greek and Roman city called Philadelphia (not the city mentioned in Revelation 3:7) was built at the same spot. Many beautiful ruins of this city remain in or near modern 'Ammān.

rabbi, rabboni. "My master"—a title of respect, especially for a religious teacher.

Rabshakeh (rab′shə kə). Title of a high Assyrian court official.

Raca (rä′kä). Insulting word; no one knows exactly what it means.

Rachel (rā′chəl). Daughter of Laban, wife of Jacob, and mother of Joseph and Benjamin. Beautiful Rachel was Jacob's first choice, but he was tricked into marrying her sister Leah first (Genesis 29:9). For many years Rachel had no children. At last she had Joseph, and then died when Benjamin was born. In some verses "Rachel" is used as a figure of speech for Jewish mothers in general (Matthew 2:16–18).

Rahab (rā′hab). Woman in Jericho who helped two Hebrew spies. She and her family were saved when the city was destroyed.

rail. To complain strongly; to speak in a rough, angry way.

raiment. Clothing; see also **change of raiment.**

Rama, Ramah (rā′mə). Name of several towns, of which these three are most important: **1.** Frontier town between Judah, the Southern Kingdom, and Israel, the Northern Kingdom (1 Kings 15:17–22; Matthew 2:18). It is now er-Ram in Jordan, 5 miles north of Jerusalem. **2.** Hometown of Samuel (1 Samuel 7:17); same as **Ramathaim-zophim** (1 Samuel 1:1). There Samuel anointed Saul as king. There David took refuge when Saul became jealous. Ramah was somewhere in the hills east of Joppa (Tel Aviv-Yafo) which are now divided between Israel and Jordan. (See also **Zuph.**) **3.** Same as **Ramoth-gilead** (2 Kings 8:29).

Ramathaim-zophim (ram′ə thā′əm-zō′-fəm). Same as **Ramah,** definition **2.**

Ramoth-gilead (rā′məth gil′i əd). Important fortress east of the Jordan River; sometimes called Ramoth or **Ramah.** King Ahab received a fatal arrow wound while trying to recapture the city. Its ruins (in northwestern Jordan) are today called Tell er Rumeith—"Hill of Ramoth."

ransom. Something given to cancel a claim against someone; that is, to **redeem** someone. Jesus gave his life as a ransom from sin and death for all who trust in him (Mark 10:45).

rase. To tear down (Psalm 137:7).

raven, ravin. To snatch, tear, and devour (Matthew 7:15).

reap. To harvest grain by hand. The reaper grasps a few stalks and cuts them off with a crude metal or flintstone scythe. See also **harvest.**

Rebecca, Rebekah (ri bek′ə). Daughter of Bethuel, sister of Laban, wife of Isaac, and mother of Esau and Jacob (Genesis 24:15). Beautiful Rebekah helped Abraham's servant to water his camels when he came looking for a wife for Isaac. After Rebekah was married, Jacob became her favorite of their twin sons. She helped him cheat his brother, trick his father, and then run away from home to escape Esau's revenge.

rebuke. To scold, blame, or reprimand.

Rechabites (rek'ə bīts). Hebrew clan that followed their forefather's advice: "Live in tents, raise no crops, and drink no wine." They may have been the same as the **Kenites.** (Jeremiah 35:2.)

recompence, recompense. 1. To reward or pay back (Romans 12: 17). **2.** Reward or payment (Hebrews 11:26).

reconcile. To make friendly again. Because of sin, there is a barrier between man and God, but Jesus Christ reconciles man to God.

recover. Besides the usual definitions, sometimes means to heal (2 Kings 5:3).

redeem. To pay a **ransom** for someone. Jesus is the redeemer—the one who provides redemption—for all who believe on him.

Red Sea. Usual translation of Hebrew words that actually mean "Reed Sea." No one is sure whether this was a name for the northern part of the Red Sea, or for a reed-filled lake. Either way, God made it possible for the Israelites to escape across this body of water when the Egyptians tried to trap them.

refrain. To hold back.

refuge. Shelter or protection; safe place to stay.

regard. To pay attention to (Luke 1: 48).

regeneration. Same as **new birth;** see also **born again.**

rehearse. To repeat in detail (Acts 14:27).

Rehoboam (rē'ə bō'əm). King of Judah, the Southern Kingdom, about 931–915 B.C. The son of mighty King Solomon, Rehoboam had an opportunity to become a great ruler also. However, he foolishly gave harsh answers when the people asked him to lower their taxes and ease their forced labor. Most of Rehoboam's people rebelled and started Israel, the Northern Kingdom. Rehoboam was left only a small, weak country to rule (2 Chronicles 9:31).

Rehoboth (ri hō'bəth). Well dug by Isaac and his servants. The name means "Room" — that is, room enough for Isaac's tribe and also for the tribes that had argued with him about water rights. There are still wells at Ruheibeh in Israel, about 19 miles southwest of Beer-sheba (Beer Sheva').

reins. Literally means kidneys (Lamentations 3:13); used as a figure of speech for one's inner thoughts and feelings, similar to the symbolic meaning of the word "heart" (Psalm 7:9).

rejoice. To be happy or make glad.

remission. Forgiveness.

remnant. Those people that are left when some disaster destroys the others; sometimes called **residue.** Hebrew prophets realized that a righteous remnant would be the only hope for their people.

rend. To tear; Hebrews sometimes tore the edges of their clothes as a sign of sorrow.

rent. Torn (Genesis 37:33); a torn place (Luke 5:36); see **rend.**

repent. 1. To feel sorry about something; to change one's mind (Genesis 6:6–7). **2.** To feel sorry for sins and turn away from them (Mark 1:15).

replenish. To fill (Genesis 1:28; 9:1).

report. Besides the usual definitions, sometimes means reputation (Acts 6:3).

requite. To pay back (Genesis 50: 15).

resemble. Sometimes means to compare (Luke 13:18).

residue. Remainder; **remnant.**

resurrection. 1. Rising from death, or coming back to life, especially the rising of Jesus (Acts 2:31). 2. Belief that human beings will live after death (Matthew 22:23).

Reuben (rōō'bən *or* rōō'bin). 1. Jacob's oldest son (Genesis 29:32). He tried to save young Joseph from their other brothers' cruel plot. 2. Tribe of Israel (Joshua 13:23); its territory extended eastward from the northern half of the Dead Sea.

Reuel (rōō'əl). Same as **Jethro.**

revelation. 1. Act of revealing or making something known (Galatians 1:12). The Bible shows how God has made himself known to people—through his wonderful universe, through the history of men and of nations, and above all, through Jesus Christ. Since the Bible tells this, it in itself is spoken of as revelation. 2. When capitalized, usually means the last book of the Bible, and the one New Testament book of Prophecy (Revelation 1:1). Revelation is also called the Apocalypse, or the Apocalypse of John. No one knows for sure which "John" was inspired to write the book: many say **John the apostle,** but some say **John the elder.** Whoever the author was, he was exiled on the Mediterranean island of Patmos and there saw marvelous visions of the past, present, and future. There are many different ideas as to what these visions mean. Everyone agrees, however, that the visions tell of God's final victory over sin and death, and of the happy results for all those who trust in God.

reverence. 1. Great love and respect (Hebrews 12:28). 2. To show great love and respect (Ephesians 5:33).

revile. To call bad names or say harsh things about (John 9:28).

reward. Besides the usual definitions, sometimes means: 1. Bribe (Psalm 15:5; Micah 7:3). 2. Punishment (Psalm 91:8).

Rhoda (rō'də). Young girl (perhaps a slave) in the household of Mary, mother of John Mark (Acts 12:13).

rid. To rescue (Genesis 37:22).

righteousness. Doing the things that one is supposed to do because of one's relationship with someone else—either God or man. A person who has a right relationship with God is supposed to do right. This is why righteousness has come to have the more general meaning of doing what is right.

right hand. Often used as a figure of speech for strength, honor, and righteousness. To sit or stand at a king's right hand means to have high honors.

rigour. Harshness or strictness (Exodus 1:13–14).

riotous. Wasteful; greedy; hoggish (Luke 15:13).

river. Often means the **Nile** (Exodus 1:22) or the **Euphrates** (1 Kings 4:21), not just any river.

road. Raid (1 Samuel 27:10 in some translations).

rock. Sometimes used as a figure of speech for God, because he is strong, firm, and unchanging (Deuteronomy 32:4; Psalm 18:2).

rod. Stick, or stick-shaped piece of metal, used for various purposes. A shepherd's rod was usually a sort of club, with rock or metal reinforcing its heavier end.

roe, roebuck (rō'buk). Small, swift, graceful deer—little more than two feet tall at the shoulder.

roll. Often means **scroll** (Jeremiah 36:2).

Roman (rō'mən). Having to do with the city of Rome, or with the

Roman Empire. The Roman Empire, which scarcely existed in Old Testament times, was the greatest world power in New Testament times. In fact, Romans ruled almost the entire known world. Few of the people conquered by the Romans were able to earn or buy the privilege of Roman citizenship. The apostle Paul's father was one of those few, and, therefore, Paul was born a Roman citizen. This is why he had the rights of fair trial, freedom from certain forms of punishment, and appeal to the emperor as the "supreme court" for Romans.

Romans. New Testament book, placed first in the section called Paul's Letters. It is the longest of Paul's writings, and includes the clearest and most detailed statement of his beliefs. Most of his other letters were written *after* he had visited the Christians he was addressing; Romans was written *before*. To his fellow believers in the great city of Rome, Paul explained that no one—whether Jew or Gentile—could save himself; that only God could save him, through Jesus Christ. He stated what kind of life Christians should live. He

shepherd with rod

mentioned some of his plans for the future—including a trip to Rome.

Rome (rōm). Capital of the Roman Empire; greatest city of New Testament times; modern capital of Italy. Built at first on seven hills beside the Tiber River, Rome expanded during its early centuries. When Paul was a prisoner there, Rome had a population of perhaps 1,200,000. Many of its great buildings of those times—some in fair condition—may still be seen today. Rome was one of the earliest centers of Christianity, and quickly became one of the most important.

room. Besides the usual definitions, sometimes means place or position (Matthew 2:22; Luke 14:7–10).

round about. All around (Mark 3: 34).

ruddy. Word used to describe a handsome boy or man (1 Samuel 16:12); probably means tanned, reddish, healthy-looking, but may also mean red-haired.

ruler of the synagogue. Leader of a group of Jews who worshiped in one particular synagogue. He made arrangements for the services, including deciding who should read the Scriptures and who should speak. Several rulers of the synagogue are mentioned in the New Testament; see **Crispus** and **Jairus.**

Ruth (rōōth). **1.** Young Moabite widow who chose to move to Bethlehem in Judah with her widowed mother-in-law, Naomi (Ruth 1:4). Later, she married Boaz and became one of the ancestors of David and of Jesus. Her love and loyalty have made her one of the favorite female characters of the Old Testament. **2.** Old Testament book of History that tells the story of Ruth, Naomi, and Boaz. No one knows who was inspired to write it. The events themselves happened during the times of the judges, but the book may not have been written till long afterward. Many people believe that the book was especially intended to show that God loves and cares for all persons—Moabites as well as Hebrews.

Sabaoth (sab'i əth). Part of a name for God; see **Lord of hosts.**

sabbath. 1. Seventh day of the week, Saturday; day of rest and worship (Exodus 20:8–11). **2.** Seven (Leviticus 25:8). **3.** Sunday, the Christian's day of worship (not used with this meaning in the Bible).

sabbath day's journey. Distance that the rules of Jewish scribes allowed a person to travel on the day of worship. It was about .6 of a mile, but could sometimes be doubled by obeying other rules.

Sabeans (sa bē'ənz). Tribe that lived in what is now Yemen; see **queen of Sheba.**

sackbut. Same as **trigon.**

man in sackcloth

sackcloth. Rough, dark clothing made of goat's hair or camel's hair and worn as a sign of sorrow or trouble.

sacrifice. Act of offering something to God; also, the offering itself. Sacrifice held a central place in Hebrew worship. The idea of giving something to God is also important in Christian worship. Sacrifice and **offering** are similar words; strictly speaking, sacrifice involves killing some animal, while offering does not. See also **burnt offering, drink offering, first fruits, meat offering, peace offering, sin offering, thank offering, trespass offering,** and **vow.**

Sadducees (saj'ə sēz). Important Jewish group that tried to keep up the traditions of the priests (as opposed to Pharisees, who tried to keep up the traditions of the prophets). The high priests and other Jewish rulers during Jesus' life were Sadducees. Sadducees believed that only the first five books of the Old Testament were really Scripture. This is one reason why they had doubts about angels, life after death, and legal interpretations of the Pharisees.

saint. Literally, someone separated or set apart from others; therefore, in the Old Testament, any true worshiper of God (Psalm 85:8); in the New Testament, any Christian (Philippians 1:1).

saith. Old form of "says" or "said."

Salamis (sal'ə mis). Port city where the first foreign missionaries first landed and preached (Acts 13: 4–5); just north of Famagusta on the eastern coast of Cyprus.

Salem (sā'ləm). Same as **Jerusalem** (at least in some passages).

Salome (sə lō'mi). **1.** Wife of Zebedee, mother of James and John, and follower of Jesus (Mark 16:1). **2.** Daughter of Herodias who asked Herod Antipas for the head of John the Baptist as a reward for her dancing. (Her name is given in a Jewish history, not in the Bible.)

Salt Sea. Same as **Dead Sea.**

salutation. Acts or words of greeting, either when meeting someone or when writing him a letter.

salute. To greet; not like a soldier's salute (Matthew 10:12).

salvation. Saving or rescue. The Hebrews saw God's salvation especially in his mighty deeds at the crossing of the Red Sea. Christians see God's salvation in the life, death, and resurrection of Jesus Christ. In one sense salvation is something now present for true believers—a rescue from sin and sorrow. In another sense salvation means that God will in the future save true believers from destruction and death.

Samaria (sə mer′i ə). **1.** Important city on a ridge about 42 miles north of Jerusalem and 25 miles east of the Mediterranean Sea. King Omri of Israel, the Northern Kingdom, bought the ridge and built his new capital on it. His son Ahab made it an even more splendid city, as did later kings. Strongly fortified, Samaria held out for three years against the most powerful army in the world at that time, but at last was conquered by Assyria in 721 B.C. Through the following centuries it was owned by many nations and partly destroyed many times. In New Testament days it was again a fine city, usually called Sebaste. Today a tiny Jordanian village called Sabasṭiyah stands on one end of the famous ridge. **2.** Area surrounding the city of Samaria and named after it— about a forty-mile square, most of which is now in Jordan. It is mostly hilly, but fertile. In New Testament times there were no guarded borders between Samaria and other areas; yet, because of bad feelings, most Jews preferred to cross the Jordan River twice rather than to travel through Samaria.

Samaritan (sə mar′ə t′n). Originally meant anyone living in **Samaria,** definition **2;** later came to mean a particular group of people, related to the Jews in family tree and in religion. (About 200 of these people still live near Mount Gerizim.) Jews of Jesus' day believed the Samaritans to be half-breeds, descended from Jews and from foreign heathen colonists. Hatred between the two groups grew through the years. This is why Jesus used several ways of pointing out that God loves and cares for Samaritans as much as for other people.

Samothrace (sam′ə thrās), **Samothracia** (sam′ə thrā′shə). Island in the Aegean Sea (now called Samothrā-ki); halfway point between Troas and Neapolis, at which Paul's ship once spent the night (Acts 16: 11).

Samson (sam′sən). Mighty Israelite hero and judge who was his own worst enemy. He won many great victories over the Philistines, but often got into difficulties—usually because of love affairs. He was finally tricked by Delilah, captured, and blinded; but as he died he succeeded in destroying more Philistines than he had ever killed before (Judges 13-16.)

Samuel (sam′yo͞o əl). **1.** Prophet and judge of Israel who anointed the nation's first two kings. Samuel was given to the Lord before his birth. He grew up helping Eli, the high priest. For many years he judged his people; but when he grew old, they asked him to name a king as his successor. God directed Samuel to anoint Saul, and later, to anoint David. Before he died Samuel asked the Israelites whether any of them could accuse him of lying or unfairness; no one could. **2.** Two Old Testament books of History, named after Samuel (although his death is told about even before the end of the first book). No one knows who was inspired to write the books; probably several persons did so. Originally the two books were part of one long scroll. First Samuel tells the stories of Samuel and Saul until their deaths, and of David before he became king. Second Samuel tells about nearly all of King David's long reign. Both books were written, not just as history or biography, but as proof of God's working in the lives of men.

Sanballat (san bal′ət). Samaritan who tried to oppose Nehemiah's work (Nehemiah 2:10).

sanctify. To make holy; to separate from ordinary things for God's use or purpose.

sanctuary. Place set aside for worship; especially, the tabernacle (Exodus 25:8) or the Temple (1 Chronicles 22:19).

sandal. A sole of wood or leather fastened to the foot by straps.

Sanhedrin (san′ə drin). Religious and political "supreme court" of the Jews in New Testament times. It was made up of 71 experts in Jewish laws. One of Jesus' trials was before the Sanhedrin; so was Stephen's trial. Perhaps Saul of Tarsus (Paul) was one of the younger members before he became a Christian. The Sanhedrin met near the Temple. In the Bible it is usually called simply "the **council.**"

Sapphira (sə fī′rə). Deceitful Christian of Jerusalem; wife of **Ananias,** definition **1** (Acts 5:1).

Sara, Sarah (sar′ə). Wife (and half sister) of Abraham; mother of Isaac. Sarah was a woman of unusual beauty, even when she was middle-aged. For many years she had no children; she even laughed at the promise that she and Abraham would begin a mighty tribe. But at last Isaac was born. Sarah died before her husband did (Genesis 11:29).

Sarai (sar′ī). **Sarah's** name at first.

Sarepta (sə rep′tə). Same as **Zarephath.**

Sargon (sär′gən). Name of several ancient kings; one of them led his Assyrian army to capture Samaria, capital of Israel, the Northern Kingdom (Isaiah 20:1).

Satan (sā′t'n). Name for the **devil.** The word actually means, "someone who opposes or hinders." In the Old Testament, the Hebrew words really say, "*the* Satan," as if this were a title. In the New Testament, Satan is used as a name.

Saul (sôl). **1.** First king of Israel. The son of Kish, a well-to-do man of the tribe of Benjamin, Saul was tall, brave, and handsome (1 Samuel 9:2.) Samuel anointed Saul as king. Saul won several victories over Israel's enemies. Soon, though, he disobeyed God's commands, became jealous of his young warrior David, and showed himself unworthy to be a ruler. Samuel warned him that another man would take his place. Saul died fighting against the Philistines on Mount Gilboa. **2.** Jewish name of **Paul.**

save. Sometimes means except, or except for (Mark 5:37).

savior, saviour. 1. Anyone who saves or brings salvation, such as the judges in Old Testament times (Nehemiah 9:27). **2.** In the Old Testament, usually means God (Isaiah 45:21). **3.** In the New

Testament, means Jesus Christ (Titus 1:4).

savour. Smell or taste.

scape goat, scapegoat. Goat that was driven away as part of a Jewish religious ceremony (see **Atonement, Day of**). All the people confessed their sins, and the animal was made a sort of representative for them. The goat then made his escape (or **scape**) and thus acted out God's taking away of the sins.

scarlet. Brilliant red dye made from certain insects; also, fine dyed cloth and clothing usually owned by wealthy people.

score. Twenty.

scourge. Whip, usually made of several cords or straps, to which were tied sharp bits of bone or metal. Scourging was a terrible form of punishment; people sometimes died from it.

scribe. 1. In the Old Testament, usually means an official of some kind (2 Kings 12:10). Scribes wrote letters, took care of legal papers, and sometimes had charge of money. **2.** In the New Testament, usually means an expert and teacher of Jewish laws (Matthew 2:4).

traveler's scrip

scrip. Wallet; traveler's bag (Matthew 10:10).

Scripture, Scriptures (skrip'chərs). Bible (John 5:39); also, any Bible verse or passage (Luke 4:21). This word is used only in the New Testament; it refers to the Old Testament—the only Bible people had at that time.

scrolls

scroll. Long roll of parchment or papyrus with writing on it; often called **roll** or **book.**

seal. 1. Ring or other ornament having a special design, meant to be pressed into soft clay or wax as one's own personal mark or brand on something (1 Kings 21:8). **2.** To press a seal into clay or wax (Daniel 6:17).

season. Sometimes means any period of time (Acts 19:22).

second coming. See **advent.**

secure. 1. Unsuspecting; off guard (Judges 8:11). **2.** To protect (Matthew 28:14).

seed. Often means descendants or family (Genesis 21:12–13).

seed time, seedtime. Time for planting **(sowing).** Wheat, barley, and flax were planted from November to January; most vegetables were planted from January to March.

seer. Prophet; literally, someone who can *see* the present and the future more clearly than other people (1 Samuel 9:9).

Seir (sē'ər). **1.** Mountain range south of the Dead Sea where Esau and his descendants (the Edomites) lived; now Jebel esh-Shera' in southern Jordan. Its name means

101

"shaggy" because it was once covered with forests; today it is bare rock. **2.** Mountain about 9 miles west of Jerusalem (now in Israel).

selah. Direction for the conductor of Hebrew music; some have thought that it means that a cymbal crash is to interrupt the chanting singers.

Seleucia (si lōō'shə). Important port and fortress city, 16 miles southwest of Antioch in Syria (now in south central Turkey). From there Paul set sail at the beginning of his first missionary journey. The harbor has filled with silt through the centuries, and is no longer usable.

Semites (sem'īts). Many groups of people, all believed to be descended from Noah's son Shem (or *Sem*), and all speaking somewhat similar languages. Among the many Semitic languages are Hebrew, Aramaic, Arabic, Canaanite, and Moabite.

Sennacherib (sə nak'ər ib). King of Assyria who tried and failed to conquer Judah, the Southern Kingdom (Isaiah 36:1).

sentence. Sometimes means judgment or opinion (Acts 15:19).

Septuagint (sep'too ə jint). Greek translation of the Hebrew Old Testament. The word means 70, because people once believed that 70 (or 72) Jewish scholars worked on the translation. This is why Septuagint is abbreviated as **LXX**—the Roman numeral for 70. The Septuagint was the first Bible translation ever made. It was the Bible Jesus knew and studied.

sepulcher, sepulchre. Grave or tomb —often a cave.

seraphim. Winged angels of some type; no one knows for sure what they were like (Isaiah 6:2,6).

serjeant. Officer of the law (Acts 16: 35,38).

Sermon on the Mount. Jesus' teachings as recorded in Matthew 5–7. No one knows for sure which mountain he sat on as he spoke. The Sermon includes many of Jesus' most famous sayings.

Sermon on the Plain. Luke 6:20–49, which sounds much like parts of the **Sermon on the Mount.**

serpent. Snake, especially a large or poisonous one.

servant. Person who works for someone else. The Bible does not al-

sepulcher

ways make it clear which servants were slaves and which received wages. A "servant of God" means someone who belongs to God and worships God. Also, in Isaiah 42–53 "servant" is used in several poetic prophecies; many people think that this "servant" is Jesus.

set at naught, set at nought. To treat as unimportant or beneath notice (Mark 9:12).

set by. Regarded as important (1 Samuel 26:24).

Seth (seth). Third son of Adam and Eve.

seven. Often used as a holy number; both seven and seventy were symbols of perfection or completeness, with no parts missing.

seven last words, seven words from the cross. Jesus' sayings during the crucifixion: (1) Luke 23:34; (2) Luke 23:43; (3) John 19:26–27; (4) Matthew 27:46; Mark 15:34; (5) John 19:28; (6) John 19:30; (7) Luke 23:46.

several. Separate or different (Matthew 25:15).

shadow of death. Deep darkness (Isaiah 9:2).

Shadrach (shad′rak). One of three young Hebrew captives in Babylon who were thrown into a blazing furnace because they would worship no one but the true God (Daniel 3).

Shalmaneser (shal′mə nē′zər). Name of several Assyrian kings, one of whom began the war that brought about the end of Israel, the Northern Kingdom (2 Kings 18:9).

shalt. Older form of "shall."

shamefacedness. Modesty (1 Timothy 2:9).

shapen. Brought into the world; born (Psalm 51:5).

Shaphan (shā′fən). Scribe and important official in the court of Josiah of Judah, the Southern Kingdom.

Shaphan and his several sons were in favor of good King Josiah's reforms. They also helped and defended the prophet Jeremiah.

shard. Same as **potsherd.**

Sharon (shar′ən). Swampy, wooded plain along the Mediterranean coast from Joppa to Mount Carmel; now in Israel. The "rose of Sharon" is a type of crocus that grows wild in this area (Song of Solomon 2:1–2).

farmer with sheaf

sheaf. Bundle of cut stalks of grain; the plural is sheaves.

Sheba (shē′bə). Area that is now Yemen; see **queen of Sheba.**

Shechem (shek′əm). Ancient, important city at the pass between Mount Ebal and Mount Gerizim, about 40 miles north of Jerusalem. It is sometimes called **Sichem** or **Sychem;** the name **Sychar** may also refer to the same place. Shechem was Abraham's first stopping place in Canaan. Jacob and his sons pastured their sheep nearby. Joshua called a meeting of the tribes there, and there Rehoboam went to be crowned king. Now only ruins remain, near still-important highways in Jordan.

sheep. Mentioned more than 500 times in the Bible, thus showing how important the raising of sheep was to people of Bible times. The type of sheep raised in Palestine

a sheepcote

has a strangely fat tail that may give several pounds of tasty mutton.

sheepcote, sheepfold. Sheep pen (John 10:1).

shekel. Measure of weight, varying from about .3 to .6 of an ounce. Sometimes gold or silver was weighed by shekels in payment, but the word "shekel" is not used to mean a coin anywhere in the Bible.

Shem (shem). Eldest son of Noah.

Shema (shə mä′). First word (in Hebrew) of Deuteronomy 6:4, which came to be the title for the confession of faith in that verse. The word means "Hear!" or "Listen!" Every Hebrew boy memorized this verse and the following verses.

Sheol (shē′ol). Name for **hell,** definition **1.**

Shephelah (shi fē′lə). Foothills between the Mediterranean coast and the mountains around and south of Jerusalem. This pleasant and fertile area stretches from near Gaza northeastward to near Joppa; most of it is now in Israel.

shepherd. Often used as a figure of speech for God or Christ; true be-lievers are the sheep that this shepherd cares for.

sherd. Same as **potsherd.**

Sheshbazzar (shesh baz′ər). Captive in Babylonia who led the first return of Jews to Jerusalem (Ezra 1:8). Some people think he was the same man as **Zerubbabel.**

shew. Old spelling of "show."

shewbread. Same as **bread of the Presence.**

shibboleth (shib′ə lith). Password once used in wartime to catch enemies who mispronounced it "sibboleth" (Judges 12:6).

shield. A piece of armor carried on the arm to protect the wearer in battle.

Shiloh (shī′lō). **1.** Name of uncertain meaning; some people think it refers to the Messiah (Genesis 49:10). **2.** Important Israelite city about 21 miles north of Jerusalem (Judges 18:31). After Joshua led the Hebrews to conquer Canaan, Shiloh became an important center of worship. The tabernacle and ark of the covenant stayed there for many years. There the boy Samuel helped Eli the priest. Not long after that, Philistine enemies captured Shiloh and destroyed the place of worship completely. The very word "Shiloh" became a warning of what might also happen to Jerusalem if God's people disobeyed him (Jeremiah 7:12–14). Today the ruins of Shiloh (in Jordan) are called Khirbat Saylūn.

Shinar (shī'när). Same as **Babylonia.**

Shishak (shī'shak). King of Egypt who invaded Judah, the Southern Kingdom (1 Kings 14:25).

shittah, shittim. Same as **acacia** (Exodus 25:5).

shoes. Usually means sandals (Mark 1:7; 6:9).

shophar (shō'phar). A horn, as of a ram, used by the Hebrews to sound battle signals or announce the beginning of religious festivals.

showbread. Same as **bread of the Presence.**

Shulamite, Shulammite (shoo'lə mīt). Title or name of a beautiful girl (Song of Solomon 6:13); no one is sure what the word means.

Shunammite (shoo'nə mīt). Woman that lives in Shunem (2 Kings 4: 12).

Shunem (shoo'nəm). Town near the valley of Jezreel (now Sūlam in Israel); best known as the home of a woman who showed hospitality to the prophet Elisha (2 Kings 4: 8).

Shushan (shoo'shən). Same as **Susa.**

Sichem (sī'kəm). Same as **Shechem.**

sickle. Curved tool for cutting grain.

Siddim (sid'im). Valley that once lay south of the Dead Sea, but is probably now under water (Genesis 14:10). The cities of Sodom and Gomorrah were probably there.

Sidon (sī'dən). Ancient Phoenician seaport on the Mediterranean; same as **Zidon.** It still exists today, as the Lebanese fishing port of Şaydā. In Old Testament times Sidon was a rich, powerful, wicked city—although sometimes overshadowed by Tyre, its former colony to the south. In New Testament times Sidon was one of the few non-Jewish areas that Jesus visited (Mark 7:24–31).

siege. Surrounding of a city by an enemy army.

sign. Something that shows outwardly some inner meaning or purpose. It may be a special miracle (John 20:30); a means of identification (Luke 2:12); a natural event (Genesis 1:14); or something else.

Sihon (sī'hän). Amorite king who fought against the Israelites on their way into the Promised Land.

Silas (sī'ləs). Christian leader at Jerusalem who became a missionary helper of both Paul and Peter; probably the same as **Silvanus** (Acts 15:22–41).

Siloam (sī lō'əm). Pool in Jerusalem, fed through a tunnel leading from a spring. Probably the pool was dug in Old Testament times, but it was first definitely mentioned in John 9:7. Part of it is still in use, in the Jordanian part of the city.

Silvanus (sil vā'nəs). Probably the same as **Silas.**

silversmith. Man who refines silver and makes things of it. There was a guild (or "union") of silversmiths in Ephesus.

Simeon (sim'i ən). **1.** Second son of Jacob, who was once imprisoned by his brother Joseph in Egypt (Genesis 42:24). **2.** Tribe of Israel that soon shrank to just a part of the tribe of Judah (Joshua 19:1). **3.** Devout old man in Jerusalem who lived to see the baby Jesus, according to God's promise (Luke 2:25). **4.** Same as **Peter** (Acts 15: 14 in some translations).

similitude. Likeness; similarity.

Simon (sī'mən). **1.** First name of **Peter** (Matthew 10:2). **2.** One of Jesus' younger half brothers (Mark 6:3). **3.** One of Jesus' twelve apostles, called the **Zealot** (Zelotes) or the Cananaean because he belonged to a political and religious party that was *zealous* (eager) to set the country free from the Romans (Acts 1:13). Nothing more is known about him. **4.** Pharisee in whose house Jesus ate supper (Luke 7:40). **5.** Healed leper of Bethany in whose house Jesus ate supper (Mark 14:3). **6.** Cyrenian (from northern Africa) who was forced to carry Jesus' cross (Luke 23:26). **7.** Magician in Samaria who tried to buy the power to work miracles (Acts 8:9); sometimes called Simon Magus. **8.** Tanner in Joppa at whose home Simon Peter stayed (Acts 9:43).

simplicity. Sincerity; lack of "showing off" (Romans 12:8).

sin. Condition of being separated from God because of wrong thoughts, attitudes, words, or deeds. The wrongs themselves are also spoken of as sins, but the condition of being a sinner means more than just breaking God's rules. It means having the whole direction of one's life turned away from what God wishes. Therefore, sin is separation from God.

Sina (sī'nə), **Sinai** (sī'nī *or* si'ni ī). **1.** Arrowhead-shaped peninsula (now belonging to the United Arab Republic) through which the Israelites traveled on their way from Egypt (Exodus 19:1). **2.** Mountain where God gave the Ten Commandments to Moses and the Israelites; same as **Horeb** (Exodus 19:11). It might have been any one of several mountains, probably in the southern tip of the Sinai Peninsula (see **1**, above). One 7500-foot peak is called Gebel Musa: "Moses' Mountain."

sin offering. Sacrifice made because a person has sinned or has broken some religious taboo. It was similar to the **trespass offering** or guilt offering, but with this basic difference: Sin offerings were made for wrongs that mainly affected the person making the sacrifice; trespass offerings were made for wrongs that mainly affected other persons to whom the sacrificer had brought harm. See also **sacrifice.**

Sion (sī'ən). In the New Testament, same as **Zion** (Matthew 21:5).

Sisera (sis'ə rə). Canaanite leader who was defeated by Deborah and Barak (Judges 4:2).

sit at meat, sit down to meat. To sit down (literally, to lie down on a couch or mat) at a table and eat (Mark 2:15).

skirt. Loose-hanging lower part of any clothing—a man's as well as a woman's (1 Samuel 24:4).

slain. Killed.

slave. Often means the same as **servant.**

slay. To kill.

slept with his fathers. Died and was buried as his forefathers had been buried.

slime. Sometimes means asphalt (Genesis 14:10 in some translations).

sling

sling. Strip of leather tied between two cords, used as a weapon. A smooth stone was placed on the leather; one cord was tied to the wrist, and the other held in the hand. The sling was "wound up" and then let go, so that the stone sped far by centrifugal force.

slothful. Lazy; slow.

sluggard. Lazy person.

smite. To strike hard; sometimes means to kill.

smitten. Past participle of "to smite."

smote. Past tense of "to smite."

snare. Trap or net.

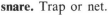

snuffer

snuffer, snuffdish. Instrument used in the tabernacle or Temple to remove the burned-out part of lampwicks.

sod, sodden. Boiled (Genesis 25:29; Exodus 12:9).

Sodom (säd'əm), **Sodoma** (säd'əm ə). City destroyed by fire because its people were so wicked. Its ruins may lie beneath the southern end of the Dead Sea. A modern Israeli town named Sedom stands nearby on the coast.

sojourn. 1. To stay for a while in a place that is not home—obeying the laws of that place and so expecting to receive proper treatment (Genesis 21:34). **2.** Period during which the Hebrews lived in Egypt.

Solomon (säl'ə mən). Son of David and third king of Israel as a united nation. Solomon's mother, Bathsheba, helped see to it that he was chosen from among David's many sons to become the new king. Reigning during the mid-years of the tenth century B.C., Solomon built upon his father's greatness. He organized the nation more efficiently, kept things mainly peaceful, and built the Temple, magnificent palaces, and strong forts. But the Bible makes it plain that Solomon was not always wise. He worked his people too hard and taxed them too heavily. By the time of his death, the kingdom was ready to split (1 Kings 2–11).

Solomon's Porch (säl'ə mənz pôrch'), **Solomon's Portico** (säl'ə mənz pôr'ti kō). Outer eastern court of the Temple in New Testament times; a beautiful walkway with high columns. Some people thought that this was the only part left of Solomon's original Temple. Actually, it was much newer than that.

sometime, sometimes. Formerly; once (Ephesians 2:13).

son of David. Sometimes used as a title for Jesus (Matthew 21:9).

Son of God. 1. In the Old Testament, means a divine being of some kind (Genesis 6:4; Job 1:6; Daniel 3:25). **2.** In the New Testament, means Jesus Christ (Mark 1:1).

Son of man. 1. In the Old Testament, means a human being (Psalm 8:4); also the coming Messiah (Daniel 7:13). **2.** In the New Testament, means Jesus (Mark 10:45).

Song of Solomon. Old Testament book of Poetry, also called Song of Songs or **Canticles.** It seems to be a collection of songs about human love and marriage. Many people have tried to explain the songs in symbols. The literal meanings, however, are probably correct. God inspired the writer to show that God is concerned about relationships between men and women, just as he is concerned about everything else in life.

sons of the prophets. Group or guild of prophets that lived and worked together (2 Kings 2:3).

soothsayer. Fortune teller (Daniel 2:27).

sop. Piece of bread dipped in gravy or stew. To dip a sop and hand it to someone was usually a way to honor that person (John 13:26).

sorcerer. Magician; wizard (Acts 13:6).

sore. Besides the usual meanings, often used to mean very much, very great, greatly, and so on (Judges 20:34; Daniel 6:14; Luke 2:9).

sought. Past tense and past participle of "to seek."

soul. Especially in the Old Testament, often means a person's whole life, being, personality—not just the part of him which is not his body. The Bible sometimes speaks of the soul as separate from the body, but it usually speaks of a person as *one* —not divided.

south, the. Sometimes means the **Negeb** (Genesis 12:9 in some translations).

sow. To plant seed; see **seedtime.**

space. 1. Time (Acts 19:8,10). **2.** Distance (Acts 5:34).

spake. Old past tense of "to speak" (Genesis 9:8).

span. Distance between the outstretched thumb and little finger; about 8–9 inches, or half a cubit.

spent. Used up (Acts 27:9).

spice. Sweet-smelling vegetable product used for cosmetics, sacred oil, perfume, burial preparations.

spikenard. Same as **nard.**

spindle. Stick with a disc onto which spun thread is wound; see **distaff.**

spirit. Life, when thought of as separate from a physical body. God is spirit (John 4:24; see also **Holy Spirit**). A human being is spirit, but also body. The Bible words for spirit, in both Testaments, are the same as the words for wind or breath. This fact makes more interesting such verses as Genesis 1:2 and John 3:8.

spoil. 1. Booty or plunder taken by a conquering army (Exodus 15:9).

2. To take as booty (Mark 3:27).

spring rain. Same as **latter rain.**

squad. Same as **quaternion.**

stablish. To establish; to set up (Psalm 148:6).

Stadion. Same as **furlong.**

staff. Long, sturdy stick—used to lean on, to fight off human and animal enemies, and so on.

stall. Sometimes used in referring to an animal that is kept penned up in its stall and fattened to make better eating; see Proverbs 15:17; Amos 6:4.

stanch. To stop bleeding (Luke 8:44).

stand to. Sometimes means to pledge one's self or agree to remain true (2 Kings 23:3).

stature. Height.

statute. Law or command.

stave. Long stick or pole.

stay. Besides the usual definitions, sometimes means: **1.** To stop, wait, or hesitate (1 Samuel 24:7). **2.** To support (1 Kings 22:35). **3.** Something or someone that supports (Psalm 18:18).

stead. Place (2 Corinthians 5:20).

steadfast, stedfast. Loyal, reliable, steady.

steadfast love. Same as **lovingkindness.**

Stephen (stē′vən). Leader of the Jerusalem church; one of the group of seven men often called the first deacons. He spoke so boldly for Christ that he became the first Christian martyr, or Christian who died for what he believed (Acts 6, 7).

steward. Person who takes charge of another person's property—especially his house, servants, and money. Christians are spoken of as stewards because everything they have actually belongs to God.

stiffnecked. Stubborn; refusing to obey. An ox stiffens his neck when the yoke on it pulls him in a direction he does not want to go.

stocks. Wooden frame with holes into which were put the ankles (and sometimes the wrists) of prisoners.

stone. To kill (or attempt to kill) by throwing stones at or on—the usual Jewish way of execution.

straightway. Immediately.

strain at. To filter or strain out (Matthew 23:24).

strait. 1. Narrow; hard to go through (Matthew 7:13). **2.** Difficult position (2 Samuel 24:14).

straiten. To shorten, cramp, or restrict (Luke 12:50).

straitly. Strictly; carefully (Acts 4: 17).

stranger. Usually means a foreign visitor, not just someone not well known (Exodus 20:10); see **sojourn.**

strawed. Spread; scattered.

stricken. Struck; hurt.

stripes. Welts, cuts, or scars from beating (Isaiah 53:5).

strong drink. Any intoxicating drink (Proverbs 20:1).

stronghold. Fortress.

stumbling block. Often used as a figure of speech for something that hinders or gets in the way (1 Corinthians 1:23).

subdue. To conquer, overcome, control.

subject to, subject unto (sub'jikt un'- too). Under the control of; obedient to (Luke 2:51).

suborn. To bribe.

substance. 1. Property; belongings (Luke 15:13). **2.** Creature; being (Genesis 7:4). **3.** Material of which something is made (Psalm 139:15–16). **4.** Assurance (Hebrews 11:1).

subtilty. Slyness; cleverness; deceit (Matthew 26:4).

suckling. Baby or young animal that is still nursing.

suffer. 1. To have or feel pain (1 Peter 2:21). **2.** To allow or let (Mark 10:14). **3.** To put up with (Matthew 17:17).

suffice. To satisfy; to be enough (John 14:8).

sumptuously. Expensively; at great cost.

sup. To eat supper.

superscription. Words written on or above something.

supplication. Request; earnest, humble asking.

surety. 1. Hostage; someone who pledges to be personally responsible for someone else's safe return, payment of a debt, or something else (Genesis 43:9). **2.** Certainty; assured fact (Acts 12:11).

Susa (soo'sǝ). Great capital city of Persia; same as **Shushan,** and now called Shush (a village in southwestern Iran). Here the story of Esther took place (Esther 1:2), and part of the story of Nehemiah (1:1).

Susanna (soo zan'ǝ). Woman who followed and helped Jesus (Luke 8:3).

sustenance. Food.

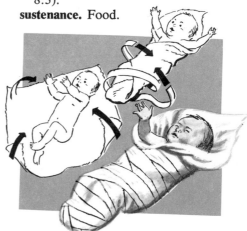

baby in swaddling clothes

swaddling clothes. Long, narrow bands of cloth wrapped around newborn babes (Luke 2:7).

swine

swine. Pig or pigs.

sycamine. Black mulberry tree, or possibly the same as **sycamore** (Luke 17:6).

sycamore, sycomore. Fig-mulberry tree; not the American sycamore. The sweet, watery fruit has to be pinched or punctured to make it ripen properly (Amos 7:14). The branches are wide and low—good for climbing (Luke 19:4).

sycamore-fig

Sychar (sī′kär). City in Samaria that Jesus visited (John 4). Some people think it is now 'Askar, in northwestern Jordan. Others think that "Sychar" was an ancient spelling for the city of **Sychem** or **Shechem.** Jacob's Well, mentioned in John 4:5–6, is by the ruins of Shechem, not at the village of 'Askar.

Sychem (sī′kəm). Same as **Shechem.**

Symeon (sim′i ən). Same as **Peter** (Acts 15:14 in some translations).

synagogue. Building where Jews gather for worship and study. Probably the idea of synagogues arose during the years when the Jews were exiles, and could not worship in Jerusalem. Even when the Temple was rebuilt, synagogues were also built in many places— 480 of them in Jerusalem itself. A synagogue was placed on the highest hill available, near water if possible, and often so that worshipers would be facing Jerusalem as they prayed. Women and children were usually allowed to come for worship services, but had to sit in a separate section or a balcony. Services included mainly prayers and the reading and explaining of Old Testament passages; see **ruler of the synagogue.** When boys became old enough to study the Scripture scrolls, they did so in a synagogue room, and a synagogue official was their teacher.

Synoptic Gospels (si näp′tik gäs′p′lz). Matthew, Mark, and Luke; "synoptic" means literally, "looking with the same eyes," and these three Gospels are much more nearly like one another than John's Gospel is like any of them.

Syria (sir′i ə), **Syrians** (sir′i ənz). Nation north of Canaan, along the Mediterranean coast and westward from it. Syria was an independent kingdom in various centuries (see **Arameans**), usually with its capital at Damascus. Syrians often fought against Hebrews, but sometimes they were allies. In New Testament times Syria was a Roman province. Today it is independent again.

Syriac (sir′i ak). Same as **Aramaic** (Daniel 2:4 in some translations).

Syrophenician, Syrophoenician (sī′rō-fi nish′ən). Person of Phoenician family, living in an area ruled by Syrians; a Gentile (Mark 7:26).

T

tabernacle. 1. Tent, booth made of poles and branches, or any other temporary shelter (Matthew 17:4). **2.** Special tent used as the Hebrews' portable place of worship (Exodus 26). Its elaborate furniture, sturdy frame, and rich curtains were made in the desert by Bezalel, Oholiab, and other workers. Here the ark of the covenant was kept. Here the priests sacrificed and prayed. No one knows whether the tabernacle wore out or was destroyed by the Israelites' enemies. By the time of King David, there seems to have been a new tabernacle in Jerusalem (2 Samuel 6:17). This was replaced by King Solomon's Temple.

Tabernacles, Feast of (fēst′ əv tab′ər-nak″lz). Same as **Booths, Feast of.**

Tabitha (tab′ə thə). Same as **Dorcas.**

table. Besides the usual meanings, sometimes means a stone tablet (Exodus 32:15–16) or a writing tablet (Luke 1:63).

Tabor (tā′bər). Hill 6 miles south-

east of Nazareth (now in Israel). Although it is less than 2,000 feet high, it stands alone overlooking the Valley of Jezreel, and so seems much taller. From Mount Tabor the judge Barak attacked Israel's enemies. Some people think the Transfiguration took place there.

tabret. Probably the same as **tambourine.**

tache. Hook or clasp (Exodus 26).

take counsel. To discuss together.

take heed. To pay attention; to be careful.

take knowledge. To notice (Acts 4: 13).

take ship, take shipping. To get into a boat.

take thought. To worry; to be anxious (Matthew 6:25).

tale. Sometimes means number or total (Exodus 5:8,18).

talebearer. Tattletale (Proverbs 26: 22).

talent. 1. In the Old Testament (and one place in the New Testament: Revelation 16:21), means a measure of weight—about 75 pounds

(Exodus 25:39). **2.** In the New Testament, means a huge sum of money—equal to what an average worker might earn in a little over 19 years (Matthew 18:24).

talitha cumi (tal′ə thə kōō′mī). Little girl, get up! (**Aramaic** words spoken by Jesus—Mark 5:41.)

Tamar (tā′mər). **1.** Daughter-in-law of Judah (Genesis 38:6). **2.** Beautiful daughter of David (2 Samuel 13:1).

tambourine

tambourine. Type of small drum that is beaten with the hand, shaken, and rattled; probably the same as **tabret** and **timbrel.** It was used in merrymaking—never in sacred music.

tare. Old form of "tore" (Luke 9:42).

tares. Weeds.

target. Sometimes means shield (1 Kings 10:16).

tarry. To wait, stay, or delay.

Tarshish (tär′shish), **Tharshish** (thär′-shish). Rich, faraway place to which Hebrew ships could sail. Its location is never made clear; probably different places are meant in different verses—from Spain in the west to India in the east.

Tarsus (tär′səs). Ancient capital city of Cilicia; now in south central Turkey. A river port, about 10 miles from the Mediterranean coast,

Tarsus is best known as Paul's hometown. In his time it was famous as a center of learning, and for linen, and goats'-hair tents produced there.

taskmaster. Overseer; boss of slaves.

tax collector. See **publican.**

Tekoa, Tekoah (tə kō′ə). Town 6 miles south of Bethlehem and 10 miles south of Jerusalem. It is best remembered as the home of Amos. Only ruins on a hilltop in Jordan mark the place today.

tell. Sometimes means to count (Psalm 147:4).

temperance. Self-control.

tempest. Storm.

tempestuous. Stormy.

temple. 1. Any house of worship (Acts 17:24). **2.** House of worship built in Jerusalem under the leadership of King Solomon (Isaiah 6:1). Probably his workmen started building about 957 B.C. and finished about 950. This Temple was not tremendously large, compared to churches of today; it was about 104 feet long, 35 feet wide, and 52 feet high. However, the building was costly and beautiful; much fine cedar-wood, olive-wood, bronze, and gold was used in construction. Rich carvings and inlays made it still more splendid. Here the people came to worship God, although only the priests could enter certain parts of the building (see **holy place** and **most holy place**). Side chambers provided room for the priests; for storage of vessels, utensils, and uniforms; and for gifts of grain and other produce. Solomon's Temple was destroyed when the Babylonians captured Jerusalem in 587 B.C. **3.** House of worship built in Jerusalem under the leadership of Zerubbabel (Zechariah 6:12). This Temple, on the exact site of

Solomon's temple

the earlier one, was probably finished about 516 B.C. It was somewhat smaller and less costly than Solomon's Temple. Here the Jews worshiped for almost 500 years. Workmen of King Herod the Great began to dismantle this Temple about 20 B.C., in order to build a finer one. **4.** House of worship built in Jerusalem under the leadership of King Herod the Great (Luke 2:46). It was mainly finished about 18 B.C., but some work on it continued throughout its history. Again, the new building was placed where the old ones had been. Herod's Temple followed the same basic plan as Solomon's and Zerubbabel's, but was far larger; its widest measurements of length, width, and height were each about 174 feet. This Temple was also much more richly decorated, and was surrounded with paved courtyards and magnificent columned porticos (such as **Solomon's Porch**). White stone and pure gold made it dazzle the eyes in sunlight. This was the Temple known to Jesus and his first followers. It was destroyed by the Romans in A.D. 70, as Jesus had predicted (Matthew 24:1–2). Today the Temple area is mainly a Moslem shrine, in the Jordanian part of Jerusalem. A few traces have been dug up of walls from the courtyards of Herod's Temple; one of these is usually called the Wailing Wall. **5.** A group of people constituting a church (1 Corinthians 3:16–17). **6.** Body of a Christian, in which the Spirit of God lives (1 Corinthians 6:19).

tempt. 1. To test someone, not necessarily with the hope that he will fail the test (Genesis 22:1; Mark 10:2). **2.** To try to get someone to do wrong (Galatians 6:1).

temptation. 1. Time just after Jesus' baptism when he went alone into the desert and there was tempted by the devil (Luke 4:13). **2.** Any time of tempting or testing (Matthew 6:13).

Ten Commandments. Great laws given by God to the Israelites of Mount Sinai; same as **Decalogue**. These are listed in Exodus 20:1–17 and Deuteronomy 5:6–21, and referred to in many other passages.

tender eyed. Weak-eyed; perhaps hav-

a tent home

ing some eye disease (Genesis 29: 17).

tenor. General meaning (Exodus 34: 27).

tent. Tents in Bible days were woven of goats' hair. Usually this was black, but faded in the sun, and therefore made the tents look striped. A curtain hung from the center pole, dividing the tent into a back room for women and a front room for men. Very rich families might have separate tents for women (Genesis 24:67). Straw mats were spread for beds, and a piece of leather for the dinner table (Psalm 23:5). Cooking was done in a hole or a crude stone oven near the tent flap.

Terah (tir′ə). Father of Abraham (Genesis 11:31–32).

teraphim. Idols belonging to a particular family (Judges 17:5); often called **images** (Genesis 31:19).

terebinth. Large tree—probably a pistachio-nut.

terrestrial. Earthly.

Tertullus (tər tul′əs). Lawyer who argued against Paul at his first trial in Caesarea (Acts 24:1).

testament. 1. Will (Hebrews 9:16–17). 2. Covenant between God and man (Hebrews 9:15). 3. Either the Old Testament or the New Testament, but more often the New.

testify. To state as true, or as proof of something.

testimony. Evidence, given in written or spoken form, of what God re-

quires of man; therefore: 1. In the Old Testament, usually means God's laws (Deuteronomy 6:17). 2. In the New Testament, usually means teaching or preaching about Jesus (Revelation 1:9).

tetrarch. Minor ruler under Roman control.

text. Actual words that were originally written in the inspired books of the Bible. Many, many ancient handwritten copies of parts of the Bible are still in existence; sometimes these are referred to as "ancient authorities." However, no original copy of any Bible book has ever been found. Therefore, scholars must study the places where handwritten copies disagree, to try to decide which were the original words. This study is called textual criticism. Difference of opinion between textual scholars is one reason why some verses read differently in different Bible translations.

Thaddaeus (thə dē′əs *or* thad′i əs). One of Jesus' twelve disciples (Matthew 10:3); same as **Lebbaeus,** and probably the same as **Judas,** definition 2.

thank offering. Sacrifice made as a way of thanking God for some unexpected gift, help, or other blessing; see **sacrifice.**

that. Besides the usual definitions, sometimes means: 1. what (Matthew 19:21); 2. so that (Luke 9: 39).

thee Old form of "you," used as the

object of a verb or preposition.

thence. There; from there.

thenceforth. From that time on.

Theophilus (thē äf'ə ləs). Man to whom Luke dedicated his Gospel (Luke 1:3) and also Acts (Acts 1:1); no one knows who he was.

thereabout. Concerning that (Luke 24:4).

thereat. At that place.

thereby. 1. By that (John 11:4). 2. Near that place (Jeremiah 51:43).

therein. In that.

thereof. Of that.

thereon. On that.

thereunto. For that (1 Peter 3:9).

therewith. With that.

Thessalonians, 1 and 2 (fŭrst' ənd sek' ənd thes ə lō'ni ənz). Two New Testament books, in the section called Paul's Letters. Many people believe that these are Paul's earliest known letters, and perhaps even the first written of any New Testament books. When Timothy brought him word that the young church at Thessalonica was doing well, Paul wrote the cheerful letter we call 1 Thessalonians. He reminded his friends that Christ would come back someday, and that in the meantime they should live as Christians ought. Perhaps this first letter was misunderstood or ignored by some of the believers, for Paul soon afterward seems to have written 2 Thessalonians. This letter stressed some of the same points as the first one, and explained how the Christians could tell for sure when a letter was from Paul and no one else.

Thessalonica (thes'ə lə nī'kə). Largest city and Roman capital of Macedonia. It had an important location for both land and sea travel: the great Via Egnatia passed through it, and it had a fine harbor on the Aegean Sea. Paul, Silas, and Timothy traveled there as missionaries, and Paul wrote two letters to the Christians of Thessalonica. The city is still an important port and naval base—now Thessaloníki in northern Greece.

thine. Older form of "your" or "yours."

think on. To think about.

third day. Jews often counted a part of a day as a whole day. When the New Testament says that Jesus was raised from death on the third day, this means that he was in the grave part of Friday, all of Saturday, and part of Sunday.

thither. There; to that place.

Thomas (täm'əs). One of Jesus' twelve disciples, also called **Didymus;** both names mean "the Twin." Thomas was brave enough to want to go to Judea with Jesus even when this might mean death, but he found it hard to believe that Jesus had actually been raised from death (John 20:27). When he saw Jesus, his doubts vanished. Only legends tell about Thomas' later life.

thou. Old form of "you," used as the subject of a verb.

Three Taverns (thrē' tav'ərnz). Stopping place on the famous Via Appia, 33 miles south of Rome (Acts 28:15).

thresh. To separate kernels of grain from the husks. This was usually done on a threshing **floor**—a large flat rock or area of beaten earth, often located at the edge of town, where the wind could more easily blow the chaff away. Men sometimes beat the grain with sticks, sometimes drove animals over it, but more often used a threshing sledge. This was a heavy wooden platform with sharp pieces of stone or metal fitted into its flat bottom. Animals pulled it back and forth across the spread-out stalks. A driver, children, or stones were sometimes used to weight down the sledge. See also **winnow** and **chaff**.

thrice. Three times.

throng. To crowd together.

throughly. Thoroughly.

Thummim (thum'mim). One of two sacred stones (the other was called **Urim**) sometimes used by the high priest in trying to find God's will (1 Samuel 14:41 in some translations; 1 Samuel 28:6). See also **lots** and **breastpiece**.

thy. Older form of "your."

Thyatira (thī'ə tī'rə). Hometown (now in western Turkey) of Lydia, and center of the manufacture of fine dyed cloth (see **purple**).

thyself. Older form of "yourself."

Tiberias (tī bir'i əs). **1.** Important city on the southwestern shore of the Sea of Galilee (John 6:23). In Jesus' day it was almost entirely a Gentile city, considered to be unclean for Jews. As far as anyone knows, Jesus never went there. Tiberias still exists as a town in northern Israel. **2.** Same as **Galilee, Sea of** (John 6:1).

Tiberius (tī bir'i əs). Roman emperor during Jesus' adult years (Luke 3:1).

tide. Time (Joshua 7:6).

tidings. News.

Tiglath-pileser (tig'lath pə lē'zər *or* tig'lath pī lē'zər), **Tilgath-pilneser** (tilgath pil nē'zər). Powerful king of Assyria and Babylonia who captured much of Israel, the Northern Kingdom (2 Kings 15:29).

Tigris (tī'gris). Great river of western Asia; called **Hiddekel** in some Bible translations (Daniel 10:4). With the Euphrates, it forms a well-watered area which was one of the birthplaces of civilization. Nineveh once stood beside the Tigris; Baghdad stands on its banks today. The river flows from Turkey through Iraq and along the border of Iran into the Persian Gulf.

till. To plow, plant, cultivate, and so on.

timbrel. Probably same as **tambourine**.

Timothy (tim'ə thi), **Timotheus** (ti-mō'thi əs). **1.** Paul's young friend and missionary helper (Acts 16:1). Half Jew, half Gentile, he lived at Lystra. Beginning during the second missionary journey, Timothy accompanied Paul for several years, ran important errands for him, and pastored churches in Paul's absence. Paul fondly spoke of him as "my own son in the faith" (1 Timothy 1:2). **2.** Two New Testament books, placed in the section called Paul's Letters. First Timothy was probably written while Timothy was pastor at Ephesus. Paul advised him on how to do his pastoral work, and warned him against false teachers. Second Timothy may have been written while Paul was a prisoner in Rome, near the time of his death. He again gave Timothy good advice, asked the younger man to come soon, and stated that he was ready to die for Christ.

Tirshatha (tūr shā'thə). Title for the governor of a Persian province (Ezra 2:63 in some translations).

Tirzah (tūr'zə). First capital of Israel, the Northern Kingdom. It was later replaced by Samaria. No one knows exactly where in northwestern Jordan Tirzah was.

Tishbite (tish'bīt). Word used to describe Elijah. Its meaning is uncertain; some people think it means the same as **Kenite**.

tithe. **1.** To give to God one-tenth of one's possessions or income (Deuteronomy 14:22). **2.** Tenth, given to God (Matthew 23:23).

tittle. Tiny ornamental mark on a letter of the alphabet.

Titus (tī'təs). **1.** Paul's friend and fellow missionary (Galatians 2:1). He seems to have been a helpful worker and an effective pastor—in Jerusalem, in Corinth, and on the island of Crete. **2.** New Testament book; eleventh in section called Paul's Letters. Paul wrote to the young pastor on Crete, advising him about church matters and warning him against false believers.

Tobiah (tō bī'ə). Ammonite who tried to oppose Nehemiah's work (Nehemiah 2:10).

toil. To work hard.

token. Sign, signal, symbol, or proof.

tolerable. Bearable; describing something that one can stand.

tongues. Often means languages (1 Corinthians 13:1), whether understood (Acts 2:11) or not understood (1 Corinthians 14:19).

Torah (tôr'ə). General Hebrew word for God's teachings; later, it came to mean just the five books of Law.

torment. Torture; pain.

touch. In the Gospels (except in Luke 11:46), always means to hold or cling to—not just to touch.

touching. Concerning (Colossians 4:10).

to wit. Namely.

town clerk. Mayor or similar high official (Acts 19:35).

tradition. **1.** Any teaching passed on from one person to another (2 Thessalonians 2:15). **2.** Rules of the Jewish scribes (Mark 7:3–13).

train. **1.** To teach (Proverbs 22:6). **2.** Group of followers or attendants (1 Kings 10:2). **3.** Long trailing robe (Isaiah 6:1).

trance. Condition of someone to whom God has given a special message in dreamlike form.

transfiguration. Event that took place on a mountain, when Jesus was changed (or *transfigured*) in the presence of three disciples; he shone with heavenly glory and talked with Moses and Elijah. Many people think that this event happened on Mount Hermon, but some say Mount Tabor.

transgression. Sin; the word literally means rebellion, or trespassing across the boundary line of right behavior.

Transjordan (tranz jôr'dən). Name sometimes given to the areas just east of the Jordan River, the Dead Sea, and the Arabah.

translate. **1.** To transfer (Colossians 1:13). **2.** To take to heaven (Hebrews 11:5). **3.** To put into another language (not used with this meaning in the Bible; all Bibles in English, of course, are translations).

travail. **1.** Very hard or painful work (Isaiah 53:11). **2.** Pains of childbirth (John 16:21).

treacherously. Disloyally; unreliably; in a tricky way.

treatise. Book that deals with some subject in much detail.

trespass offering. Sacrifice offered (usually of a ram but sometimes of a male lamb) when someone has in some way harmed another person; same as **guilt offering.** See also **sin offering** and **sacrifice.**

tribe. Any group of related families; in the Bible, almost always means the descendants of one of Jacob's sons or grandsons.

tribulation. Great trouble or suffering.

tribune. Roman military officer; commander of a **cohort;** same as **chief captain.**

tribute. Forced payment, as from a defeated nation to its conqueror (2 Kings 23:33; Mark 12:14).

trigon. Type of lyre or harp, probably having seven strings; same as **sackbut.**

Trinity. Three **persons** of God, or three ways that God has made himself known—all combined in the one being of God. The three persons are God the Father, God the Son (Jesus Christ), and God the Spirit (Holy Spirit). The Bible does not use the word "trinity," but suggests it in such verses as Matthew 28:19.

triumphal entry. Jesus' ride into Jerusalem, described in Matthew 21:1–11; Mark 11:1–11; Luke 19:28–44; John 12:12–19.

Troas (trō'as). Large Asian seaport, built near (and named after) ancient Troy. It was such an important city that Roman emperors considered moving their capital from Rome to Troas. Paul passed through Troas several times and preached there. Only ruins (in northwestern Turkey) remain today.

trow. To think.

trump, trumpet (trum'pit). **1.** Curved horn of a ram or antelope, blown as a signal (Joshua 6:4). It was really a noisemaker rather than a musical instrument, and was rarely used with musical instruments. **2.** Straight horn, about two feet long, made of metal, bone, or shell (Numbers 10:2). This type of trumpet could play several different notes, and was much used by priests in religious music.

try. To test, as metal is tested for purity and value (Psalm 139:23).

tumult. Uproar; confusion; loud noise.

turtle. Turtledove (Song of Solomon 2:12).

twain. Two; both.

twelve. Important number to the Hebrews, because there were twelve tribes of Israel. When Jesus chose **twelve** disciples, this was a way of saying, "I am starting a new people of God, just as the old people of God were begun with twelve men." When the New Testament says "the twelve," it means these first disciples.

Tyrannus, hall of (hôl' əv tī ran'əs), **school of Tyrannus** (skōōl' əv tī-ran'əs). Lecture hall or schoolroom at Ephesus in which Paul preached for two years; it may have been lent or rented. (Acts 19:9.)

Tyre (tīr). Ancient Phoenician seaport, famous for its wealth, wickedness, and bold sailors. Queen Jezebel of Israel, the Northern Kingdom, was a Tyrian princess. Probably founded as a colony of Sidon, Tyre itself started another famous colony: Carthage. Through the centuries few enemies could capture Tyre, mainly because it stood on a rocky island half a mile off the coast. Alexander the Great built the land out to it, however, and conquered the proud city. Tyre has never been as great since, and today is a small Lebanese town called Ṣūr.

priest with trumpet

Unawares. Without realizing it.

uncircumcised, uncircumcision. See **circumcise** and **circumcision.**

unclean. See **clean.**

unction. Anointing.

under colour. Pretending (Acts 27: 30).

unfeigned. Real; genuine.

unforgivable sin. Rejecting Christ and refusing to recognize that his work is God's work (Mark 3:29–30); same as **unpardonable sin.**

unicorn. Wild ox (Job 39:9–10).

Unleavened Bread, Feast of. Same as **Passover.**

unpardonable sin. Same as **unforgivable sin.**

unrighteousness. Opposite of **righteousness;** not just wickedness in general.

unspeakable. Inexpressible; hard to describe because it is so great.

untoward. Troublesome; stubborn; crooked.

upbraid. To scold.

uphold. To hold up.

upper room. Large houses in Bible times often had a big room (see **guest chamber**) on the second floor (Acts 9:37–39; 20:8), or on the flat roof (2 Kings 4:10). Usually "upper room" means the place in Jerusalem where Jesus ate the Last Supper with his disciples (Luke 22: 12). Possibly this was the same room as the one in which Jesus' followers later met (Acts 1:13); some people think it was in the home of Mary, John Mark's mother (Acts 12:12).

upright. Just and honest.

Ur (ur), **Ur of the Chaldees** (ûr'əv thə kal'dēz). Great and ancient city of Babylonia; first home of Abraham. Archaeologists have dug out large two-story homes, harbors for river-boats, and a huge temple-tower with ramped sides, used for worship of the moon god. In Abraham's times the Euphrates flowed by the city; today the ruins of Ur (in southeastern Iraq) are several miles from the river's newer channel.

Uriah (yoo rī'ə). Name of several Old Testament men; the best known is a brave Hittite warrior (1 Chronicles 11:41) whom King David allowed to be killed in battle, so that David could marry Uriah's beautiful wife, Bathsheba.

Urim (oor'im). See **Thummim** and **lots.**

usury. Lending money for interest; also, the interest itself. Sometimes a high or unfair rate of interest was charged.

utmost, uttermost. Farthest; highest; greatest; most that is possible.

Uz (uz). Desert area somewhere east of the Jordan River; the Bible does not give its exact location.

Uzzah (uz'ə). Man who died while trying to bring the ark of the covenant to Jerusalem (see 2 Samuel 6).

Uzziah (ə zī'ə). Great and good king of Judah, the Southern Kingdom (2 Chronicles 26:1). During his reign, beginning about 784 B.C., he won military victories, improved agriculture, and strengthened national defense. Uzziah became a leper when he tried to become priest as well as king; his son Jotham was regent during his last years. However, Uzziah was still remembered as the strongest king in Jerusalem since Solomon.

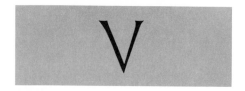

vail. Same as **veil.**

vain. Empty; useless (1 Corinthians 15:14).

vainglory. Pride; conceit (Philippians 2:3).

vale. 1. Valley (Genesis 37:14). 2. Same as **Shephelah** (Deuteronomy 1:7).

valley. Sometimes means the same as **Shephelah** (Joshua 11:16).

valor, valour. Courage.

vanity. Emptiness; worthlessness; uselessness (Acts 14:15). The Bible word never means conceit or false pride.

variableness. Variability; changeability.

variance. Disagreement; quarreling.

Vashti (vash′tī). Queen of King Ahasuerus of Persia (Esther 1:9); she was replaced by Queen Esther.

vaunt. Boast; brag.

vehement. Strong; hot.

veil. Same as **vail.** 1. Article of clothing—sometimes one that covered

much more than the face (Ruth 3:15 in some translations). 2. Richly embroidered curtain that hung in front of the **most holy place** in the tabernacle or the Temple. Only the high priest could go behind it. The veil of the Temple was torn in two when Jesus died (Mark 15:38).

vengeance. Usually means punishment for wrong done (see **avenge**) rather than revenge (Acts 28:4). Such punishment was sometimes done by men (see **avenger**), sometimes by God (Romans 12:19).

venison. Meat from wild game (Genesis 27:5); not necessarily deer meat.

verily. Truly.

verity. Truth.

version. Something translated from the language in which it was first written. Since the Bible was written in Hebrew, Aramaic, and Greek, all Bibles in English are versions.

vessel. Anything hollow, used for holding something; sometimes a figure of speech for a person into whom God pours his strength and guidance (Acts 9:15).

vestment, vesture (ves′chər). Article of clothing.

vex. To cause great trouble; not just to annoy (Acts 12:1).

victuals. Food.

vile. Sometimes means lowly or shabby (James 2:2), not evil.

village. Small settlement with no city walls (1 Samuel 6:18); not a **fenced city.**

vine. Nearly always means grapevine.

vinegar. Since vinegar was made from spoiled grape wine, it is sometimes hard to know whether the Bible means true vinegar or sour wine. Both were much used. Bread dipped in vinegar was considered tasty (Ruth 2:14). Sour wine was sometimes drugged and given to crucified criminals to ease their pain (Matthew 27:34,48).

vineyard. Since grapes were a main crop in Bible times, vineyards are often mentioned. Sometimes a vineyard (Isaiah 5:1–7) or a vine (John 15:1–5) was used as a figure of speech to teach something about God's relationship with men.

viol. Same as **harp.**

viper. Poisonous snake.

virgin. 1. Any woman who has never had sexual relations (Genesis 24: 16). **2.** Jesus' mother (Luke 1:27); see **Mary,** definition **1.**

virgin birth. Jesus' birth to the virgin Mary by a special miracle of God.

virginity. Condition of being a virgin, or time when a woman is still a virgin.

virtue. Sometimes means power rather than goodness (Luke 6:19; 8:46).

visage. Face.

vision. Usually means the method used by God for showing something that cannot otherwise be known—a special message to a person's (often a prophet's) mind.

visit, visitation (viz'ə tā'shən). Besides the usual definitions, sometimes means God's action in coming to someone, bringing help or punishment as needed (Exodus 20:5; Luke 1:68; 7:16; 19:44).

void. Empty; open.

vow. Solemn promise made to God— sometimes a promise to make a particular **sacrifice,** called a votive offering.

wail. To show sadness or pain by loud, long cries.

wait. To "wait for God" means to remain true to him, while eagerly ex-

pecting him to bring help, salvation, or some other blessing (Isaiah 40: 31).

walk. Sometimes used as a figure of speech for one's whole conduct or way of life (Acts 9:31).

ward. Guard or custody (Genesis 40: 3–4; Acts 12:10).

wast. Older form of "were," used with "thou."

waste. Besides the usual meanings, often means ruined (Nehemiah 2: 3).

watch. Besides the usual definitions, sometimes means: **1.** Guard (Matthew 27:65–66). **2.** To stay awake (Matthew 26:40–41). **3.** One of three (Hebrew) or four (Roman) equal shifts into which sentries divided the night (Mark 6:48).

guard on watchtower

watchtower. Round stone building about 10 feet tall, from which a farmer guarded his crops against men or animals.

Water Gate. Gate in the city wall on the eastern side of Jerusalem; probably close to a spring (Nehemiah 8:1,3).

wax. To grow or increase.

Weeks, Feast of. Harvest thanksgiving festival of the Hebrews; same as **Pentecost** (Deuteronomy 16:9–10). In May, when wheat harvest began, loaves made from the new grain were offered as a sacrifice (which, in this case, was eaten by the priests). Another feature of this happy celebration was a public meal to which poor people and foreigners were invited.

well. Rain is scarce in Bible lands; it is no surprise to find water wells mentioned in the Bible more than sixty times.

wert. Older form of "were," used with "thou."

whence. From where; where.

whereas. Because.

whereby. By which; with which.

wherefore. 1. Why (Matthew 9:4). **2.** Therefore (Hebrews 12:1).

whereinto. Into which.

whereof. Of which.

whereunto. 1. To what (Luke 13:18). **2.** Concerning which; about which (1 Timothy 6:12).

whereupon. At which; after which.

wherewith (with'), **wherewithal. 1.** With which (Ephesians 6:16). **2.** That with which (Luke 17:8).

whether. Sometimes means which (Mark 2:9).

whiles, whilst. While (Matthew 5:25; Psalm 141:10).

whit. Least bit.

whither. Where.

whithersoever. Wherever.

whole. Besides the usual definitions, sometimes means well or healthy (Luke 7:10).

widow. Woman who has lost her husband. Hebrew law did not ordinarily allow a widow to inherit her husband's property. This is why widows are often mentioned as unfortunate people whom true followers of God should love and care for.

wilderness. Area that is not cultivated, and not lived in permanently; it may be desert, or may have considerable vegetation.

wiles. Clever tricks.

wine. Grape wine was a common drink in Bible lands; pure water was scarce, and milk spoiled quickly without refrigeration. The Bible warns often against drinking too much wine (Proverbs 23:30–31).

winefat, winepress, wine vat. Two pits, usually hewed into rocky ground, and connected by a channel; sometimes called **press.** Grapes were poured into the larger and shallower pit, and stamped on by human feet, to make juice flow through the channel into the smaller and deeper pit.

wink at. To overlook (Acts 17:30).

winnow. To separate threshed grain from straw and chaff. A man would go to his threshing **floor** in the late afternoon and evening, when the

winnowing grain

wind would usually be blowing (Ruth 3:2). As he would throw up the stalks with a pitchfork or shovel, the grain would drop at his feet, and the straw a short distance off; but the chaff would be blown away. See also **chaff** and **thresh.**

wisdom. Quality of God by which he is able to create and control all things; quality of human beings by which they are able to live successful lives. Many parts of the Bible (especially the Old Testament) have wisdom as their subject. The books of Job, Proverbs, and Ecclesiastes are often called "wisdom literature."

Wise Men. Men who came from some unnamed eastern country to worship little Jesus; same as **Magi.** Probably they were Persian priests who worked sacred magic and studied the stars to learn of coming events.

wist. Knew (Luke 2:49).

wit. To know (Exodus 2:4).

withal. In addition (1 Samuel 16:12).

withered. When referring to all or part of a person's body, means deformed, twisted, or weak (Luke 6: 6–8).

within. Inside.

without. Besides the usual definition, often means outside (John 18:16).

withstand. To resist.

witness. Someone who has firsthand knowledge of something. Christians are commanded to be witnesses of what they know about Christ. Because so many of Jesus' first faithful witnesses were killed, the New Testament Greek word for witness has become our English word martyr.

woe. Great sorrow or trouble; often used as an exclamation, meaning "Alas!" or "How terrible!"

womb. Uterus; hollow organ in a mother's body inside which a baby grows till birth.

wondrous. Wonderful.

wont (wunt). Accustomed; habit (Acts 16:13).

word. Besides the usual definitions, often used to refer to any means by which God makes his will known to people; therefore: **1.** God's message through the preaching of a prophet (Hosea 1:1). **2.** God's message through his written laws (Psalm 119:105). **3.** Preaching by or about Jesus (Mark 4:33; Acts 4:29). **4.** Jesus Christ himself (John 1:1,14).

world. Besides the usual definitions, sometimes (especially in the New Testament) means period of time in which life exists as we know it —not eternity (Luke (18:30; Galatians 1:4; Ephesians 1:21).

wormwood

wormwood. Bitter-tasting plant (Amos 5:7).

worship. To show reverence for. Some of the Old Testament words translated "worship" mean literally "to bow down." Some of the New Testament words mean "to kiss the hand." Both ideas came from ways kings were honored in those times. In two verses (Acts 16:14; 18:7), "worshiping God" means obeying Old Testament rules of conduct, without actually becoming a Jew in religion.

wot. To know (Genesis 44:15).

123

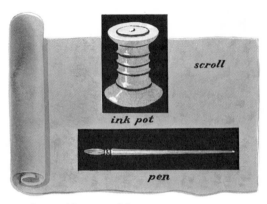

ancient writing materials

would God, would to God. Usually an exclamation: "If only it could be!" or "Oh, that it could be!"

wrath. Great anger.

wrest. To twist.

writing. From very early Bible times the art of writing was known. Words were written sometimes on stone (Deuteronomy 27:2–3); sometimes on wood (Ezekiel 37:16); sometimes on papyrus (2 John 12); sometimes on metal, clay, broken bits of pottery, leather, or parchment. Sometimes a stylus was used (Jeremiah 17:1), sometimes a pen or brush (Psalm 45:1) and ink (3 John 13).

Writings. One of the three main divisions of the Hebrew Bible. (The others are **law** and **prophets.**) It includes Ruth, 1 and 2 Chronicles, Ezra, Nehemiah, Esther, Job, Psalms, Proverbs, Ecclesiastes, Song of Solomon, Lamentations, and Daniel. This was the last part of the Old Testament to be recognized as Scripture.

wroth. Angry.

wrought. Made.

Yahweh (yä′wǝ *or* yä′we). Hebrew personal name of the true God— the Lord God of the Old Testament and the Father of our Lord Jesus Christ; same as **Jah, Jehovah,** and **"Lord,"** definition **3.** Yahweh was the name God used when he made his covenant with the Israelites. Because the name was considered too sacred to be spoken, a word meaning "Lord" was often substituted for it. When the Old Testament prints "LORD" in capitals, this nearly always means Yahweh. "Jehovah" is used in some translations, but "Yahweh" is much closer to the original form of the name. "Yahweh" has something to do with the Hebrew verb "to be" (see Exodus 3:13–15); it may mean "I am," "I will be," or "I cause to be."

124

ye. Older form of "you" as a plural pronoun.

yea. Yes; truly.

year. Hebrews had no definite calendar as people do today. During some periods of history, they celebrated new year's at the beginning of spring; during other periods, at the beginning of autumn. Events were often dated by the year of the reign of a king.

yesternight. Last night.

yield. **1.** To produce, give, bear (Psalm 67:6). **2.** To give up; to surrender (Romans 6:13).

yield up the ghost. To die (Matthew 27:50).

yoke. **1.** Wooden frame laid across the shoulders of two oxen so that they can pull something (1 Samuel 6:7). **2.** Pair (Luke 14:19). **3.** State of being imprisoned or harshly treated, whether or not something like an actual yoke is used (1 Kings 12:4). **4.** State of being a pupil or learner (Matthew 11:29–30).

Zacchaeus, Zaccheus (za kē'əs). Rich tax collector in Jericho who became a follower of Jesus (Luke 19:1–10).

Zacharias (zak'ə rī'əs). Father of John the Baptist (Luke 1:5); a priest; same as **Zechariah,** definition 3.

Zadok (zā'dok). High priest in the times of David and Solomon; his descendants became the main family of priests.

Zarephath (zar'ə fath). Phoenician seacoast town where Elijah stayed for a while with a poor widow and her son; same as **Sarepta.** Today a Lebanese town a few miles inland bears the name Aş Şarafand.

zeal. Enthusiasm; strong, eager feeling.

Zealot (zel'ət). Member of a religious and political party in Jesus' times; same as **Cananaean** and **Zelotes.** (See also **Simon,** definition 3.) Zealots hoped to free their country from the Roman Empire.

zealous. Enthusiastic; eager; having strong feelings.

Zebedee (zeb'ə dē). Father of James and John, two of Jesus' twelve disciples (Matthew 4:21); apparently he was a fisherman of some wealth: he had servants.

Zebulon (zeb'yə lən). A son of Jacob; tribe of Israel occupying territory west of the Sea of Galilee.

Zechariah (zek'ə rī'ə). Name of dozens of Bible characters, including one king; the most important, however, are these: **1.** Prophet of Jerusalem who was active about 520–518 B.C. (Zechariah 1:1). Like Haggai, he encouraged the people to rebuild the Temple. **2.** Old Testament book of the Minor Prophets, written (at least in part) by the prophet Zechariah. It says much about the new Temple and about the coming of the Messiah. Zechariah 9:9 is a prophecy that came true in Jesus' triumphal entry into Jerusalem. **3.** Same as **Zacharias.**

Zedekiah (zed'ə kī'ə). **1.** False prophet who opposed the prophet Micaiah (1 Kings 22:11,24). **2.** Last king of Judah, the Southern Kingdom (2 Kings 24:17). He often asked advice of the prophet Jeremiah, and seemed to mean well, but he was too weak and wishy-washy to do right. Finally Babylonia conquered his kingdom in 587

B.C. and led him away as a blinded captive.

Zelotes (zi lō′tēz). Same as **Zealot.**

Zephaniah (zef′ə nī′ə). **1.** Prophet during the time of King Josiah of Judah, the Southern Kingdom (Zephaniah 1:1); probably he was Josiah's distant cousin. He lived and preached in Jerusalem. **2.** Old Testament book of the Minor Prophets. Zephaniah saw the wickedness of some of his people who were worshiping false gods. Then (about 630–625 B.C.) there came an invasion of the Scythians, a fierce tribe. Zephaniah saw this as a warning of far worse things that God would cause to happen, unless his people turned away from their sins.

Zerubbabel (zi rub′ə bəl). Captive in Babylonia who returned to Jerusalem as governor and led in the rebuilding of the Temple about 520–515 B.C. (Ezra 2–4). Some people think he was the same man as **Sheshbazzar.**

Zeus (zoōs). Greek name for the supreme ruler of the gods; similar to the Roman god **Jupiter** (Acts 14:12).

Ziba (zī′bə). Servant of King Saul, and later of Saul's grandson, the lame prince Mephibosheth (2 Samuel 9:2).

Zidon (zī′d′n). Same as **Sidon.**

Ziklag (zik′lag). City southwest of Jerusalem that David used as a base of operations during the time he was friendly with the Philistines. Once Amalekites raided it in David's absence, and he had to chase them to recover his people and possessions. Ruins of Ziklag probably lie near the Jordanian border of Israel, east of Gaza.

Zion (zī′ən). Name for part or all of Jerusalem; same as **Sion** (in the New Testament). Originally the name meant the southeastern hill, the oldest part of the city. Later, it came to include the northeastern hill, on which the Temple was built. Still later, it meant the entire city. After Bible times the name Zion was given to the southwestern hill in the older part of Jerusalem.

Zipporah (zip′ə rə). Moses' wife (Exodus 2:21).

Zuph (zuf *or* zoōf). Place where Saul searched for his father's lost donkeys (1 Samuel 9:5); probably the area around **Ramah,** definition **2.**